# THE FALL OF TH
# ROMAN REPUBLI

*The Fall of the Roman Republic* provides an accessible introduction to this complex topic in Roman history. Drawing on a wealth of recent scholarship, David Shotter examines how the Roman republic was destabilised by the unplanned growth of the Roman empire. Key topics discussed include:

- The government of the republic
- How certain individuals took advantage of the expansion of the empire
- Julius Caesar's rise to power
- The emergence of the Augustan principate following Julius Caesar's murder.

This new second edition has been revised throughout to take into consideration the latest research in the field. Additions also include an expanded and updated guide to further reading and an index.

**David Shotter** is Professor Emeritus in Roman Imperial History at the University of Lancaster. His many books include *Rome and Her Empire* (2003), *Tiberius Caesar* (2nd edition, 2004), *Nero* (2nd edition, 2005) and *Augustus Caesar* (2nd edition, 2005).

# LANCASTER PAMPHLETS IN ANCIENT HISTORY

GENERAL EDITORS: ERIC J. EVANS AND P.D. KING

Hans Pohlsander, *Emperor Constantine*
David Shotter, *Augustus Caesar*
David Shotter, *The Fall of the Roman Republic*
David Shotter, *Nero*
David Shotter, *Roman Britain*
David Shotter, *Tiberius Caesar*
Richard Stoneman, *Alexander the Great*
John Thorley, *Athenian Democracy*
Sam Wilkinson, *Caligula*

# THE FALL OF THE ROMAN REPUBLIC

## Second Edition

David Shotter

Routledge
Taylor & Francis Group

LONDON AND NEW YORK

First published
1994 by Routledge
2 Park Square, Milton Park, Abingdon, Oxon OX14 4RN

Simultaneously published in the USA and
Canada by Routledge
711 Third Avenue, New York, NY 10017

Second edition published 2005

*Routledge is an imprint of the Taylor & Francis Group, an informa business*

© 1994, 2005 David Shotter

Typeset in Garamond and Scala by RefineCatch Limited, Bungay, Suffolk

British Library Cataloguing in Publication Data
A catalogue record for this book is available from the British Library

Library of Congress Cataloging in Publication Data
A catalogue record has been requested

ISBN10: 0–415–31939–0 (hbk)
ISBN10: 0–415–31940–4 (pbk)

ISBN13: 978 0–415–31939–3 (hbk)

ISBN13: 978 0–415–31940–9 (pbk)

# CONTENTS

LIST OF FIGURES                                                        vi
FOREWORD                                                               vii
ACKNOWLEDGEMENT                                                        viii

**Introduction**                                                       1

1 **The government of the republic**                                   5

2 **The growth of empire**                                             19

3 **The political temperature rises: the Gracchi, Marius
  and Sulla**                                                          30

4 **The rise and domination of Pompey**                                46

5 **The 'three-headed monster' and the slide to civil war**            64

6 **The dictatorship of Julius Caesar**                                79

7 **The final act: Antonius, Octavian and Lepidus**                    90

**Epilogue**                                                           98

APPENDIX I  PRINCIPAL DATES                                            103
APPENDIX II  MAGISTRACIES OF THE ROMAN REPUBLIC                        106
APPENDIX III  THE VOTING ASSEMBLIES OF THE REPUBLIC                    110
APPENDIX IV  THE PROVINCES OF THE ROMAN EMPIRE                         112
SELECT BIBLIOGRAPHY                                                    114
INDEX                                                                  119

# FIGURES

1   Legislation in Rome after 287 BC                                    17
2   Stemma showing the links between the Scipiones,
    Claudii and Sempronii Gracchi in the second century BC    32
3   The Roman empire in the late-first century BC                   48

# FOREWORD

Lancaster Pamphlets offer concise and up-to-date accounts of major historical topics, primarily for the help of students preparing for Advanced Level examinations, though they should also be of value to those pursuing introductory courses in universities and other institutions of higher education. Without being all-embracing, their aims are to bring some of the central themes or problems confronting students and teachers into sharper focus than the textbook writer can hope to do; to provide the reader with some of the results of recent research which the textbook may not embody; and to stimulate thought about the whole interpretation of the topic under discussion.

# ACKNOWLEDGEMENT

My thanks are due to my wife, Anne, for her assistance in the preparation of this manuscript.

# INTRODUCTION

The English word 'republic' is derived from two Latin words (though often written as one): *res publica*; the term does not in itself imply any very specific form of government, except in so far as its meaning (in translation) is 'the public concern'.

The Romans applied the term to their state over a lengthy period, although modern students of Roman history tend to restrict its application to the period between the ending of the ancient monarchy (in the late-sixth century BC) and the inauguration by Augustus Caesar, after his defeat of Marcus Antonius in 31/30 BC, of a new monarchy (commonly called the 'principate'). Romans themselves distinguished between these two phases of their governmental life by referring to the Augustan system as *respublica* and to its predecessor as *vetus respublica* ('the old republic'). Despite this, however, we should not underestimate the perceived differences between the two systems – not just in the nature of government itself, but also, as Cornelius Tacitus pointed out, in the matter of historians' access to information. This he regarded as having been much more straightforward during the 'old republic' than was the case with its successor.

This short account is, therefore, concerned with the 'old republic' and, in particular, with that period of it following the first of Rome's three wars against the Carthaginians (264–241 BC); this period saw Rome rising to unprecedented heights of power and influence in the Mediterranean, but undermining her own political institutions with the burdens and responsibilities incurred in maintaining her empire. It is little wonder that it has been commonly asserted in one way or another that it was the growth of the Roman empire that 'broke' the republic: such a perception characterises 'the fall of the Roman republic' as essentially a period of great change – political, social, military and economic. However, whilst it would not be reasonable to claim that the Roman governing class was uniformly opposed to change, it was a commonly held conviction that conservatism was sound and that the *respublica* should not be allowed to slip back into monarchy (*dominatio* by an individual or a group).

*Libertas* ('liberty') is commonly found in ancient writers used as a synonym for *respublica*; *dominatio* was the undermining, even absence, of *libertas*. These two terms, and what they stood for, represent constant themes in any study of the 'old republic'. The republic had, after all, represented in its origin a reaction against *dominatio*: although there is much that remains uncertain regarding the circumstances, chronology and nature of the republic's foundation, it seems clear that its 'founding-fathers' were anxious to prevent the Roman state from succumbing to the arbitrary whim of one man. It may also have been a reaction on the part of a patrician aristocracy which was largely landowning against the industrial and commercial entrepreneurism that may have driven a number of Rome's kings. The republic's system of government was constructed in such a way, therefore, as to contain adequate checks to prevent this: the plurality of offices and the collegiality of most of them, together with the principles of consultation and of having to account for one's tenure of office, were amongst the most important of these. In the first place, however, the establishment and maintenance of the constitutional and territorial integrity of the fledgling state must have been the most urgent considerations.

Categorising the Roman republic has never proved to be a straightforward undertaking: nor was it static over the five centuries of its existence. It changed to accommodate new situations – perhaps not always with sufficient decisiveness – and it bowed to pressures. It is clear that it was neither a monarchy, nor an oligarchy, nor again a democracy; yet it encapsulated elements of all of these. Its attraction to a Greek thinker, such as Polybius (*c.* 208–125 BC), who came to Rome as a prisoner-of-war and became an intimate of a number of senatorial families (including the Scipiones), was that it seemed to have brought an end to the cycle of instability which had dogged Greek city-states, as they moved, apparently endlessly, from monarchy to aristocracy to democracy and back to monarchy. Polybius (*Histories* VI.1–18) admired the Roman republic because it brought together elements of all of the traditional constitutional types into a 'mixed constitution', which was made up of executive officers (the magistrates), an aristocratic council (the senate) and popular assemblies. None of these could operate entirely on its own, but required the co-operation of the other two.

It was at one time customary to dismiss any notion of demo-cracy in the Roman republic, but to see it as a state run by and for a small group of aristocratic families: yet, if this really was the case, what was the purpose of that great Roman institution, polit-ical oratory, if not to sway and convince to a point of view? Nor, surely, can democracy be denied in a state in which final political decisions were made by popular assemblies. As the historian Cornelius Tacitus showed in the opening sentences of his *Annals*, monarchic 'episodes' during the period of the republic were rare and related to particular crises. In normal circumstances, it remained one of the harshest forms of political criticism to accuse an individual or a group of attempting to establish a *regnum* ('kingship').

The purposes of the present study are, first, to examine the route of the Roman republic to political stability, and how it extended its influence first over Italy and then into the wider Mediterranean world; this will serve as a base for understanding how the edifice gradually showed itself unable to survive its growth without such major modifications as those that were to characterise the reigns of the first emperor, Augustus, and his successors.

Augustus himself, in his long reign of nearly half-a-century (31 BC–AD 14), highlights a consideration that is of crucial importance in the present study: the republic was a great deal more than a set of governmental institutions; it embraced centur-ies of accumulated tradition, together with the societal bonds of law and religion. It was, in short, the history of 'the Roman senate and people' (*senatus populusque Romanus*), words which provide perhaps the most evocative initials of European history – SPQR.

Augustus' reign represented the culmination of a process which occupied the last century of the republic, in which with increasing frequency individuals showed by their behaviour that a return to some kind of centralised supervision of the republic and its empire had become the soundest recipe for continued stability. Such individuals did not generally rise (or fall) without struggle and turmoil, as is shown by the careers of men such as the Gracchus brothers, Marius, Sulla, Pompey, Caesar and finally Octavian (Augustus) himself. 'So great a task was it to found the City of Rome' – equally so, for it to survive and grow.

# 1

## THE GOVERNMENT OF THE REPUBLIC

Roman society was classified into two groups (or 'orders') – patricians and plebeians; the origins of this classification are obscure and, over the years, various explanations have been suggested. These include an original racial difference between the two groups, or a distinction based upon the concepts of economic success or failure. As we have seen, doubts persist over the chronology of the ending of the antique monarchy and the inception of the republic. But if we accept the traditional dating of *c.* 509 BC, then, despite the usual assertion that the early republic saw a patrician monopoly of power and influence, it must be noted that plebeians, too, held prominent positions until the middle years of the fifth century BC. It may be that so long as Rome remained within the Etruscan cultural and economic sphere there was opportunity still for those whose wealth was based upon sources other than agricultural.

However, by *c.* 460–450 BC, the changing tenor of social and economic life in Rome appears to have shifted the political bias in favour of landowning patricians who, from that time, seem to have exercised the dominant role. According to Roman tradition, the period between the mid-fifth century BC and the early-third saw changes take place within a process known to history as the 'Struggle of the Orders'. Again, it is not easy to assess the character of this, except to note that, as a result, plebeians won social concessions such as the right of intermarriage with patricians, and political advance through the winning of access to senatorial membership and to office-bearing, as well as gaining sovereignty for 'their body', the Assembly of the Plebeians (*concilium plebis*). How much of a change such 'concessions' represented, however, remains uncertain because the ability to participate fully in government must have continued to depend upon wealth. Large numbers of plebeians must simply have been too poor for such changes to have had much meaning for them, whilst those who became sufficiently wealthy to participate in a meaningful way must have come to identify their interests more closely with those of the patricians. In that sense, the 'Struggle of the Orders' must in essence have led to a revised polarisation in Roman society.

It is reasonable to suppose that the physical growth of the Roman state between the fifth and third centuries broadened the wealth-base. Thus, the governing aristocracy of Rome evolved into a combined group of patricians and plebeians wealthy enough to sustain the burdens of power and office, and of course to grasp the opportunities offered by them. Thus, from the third century BC, this governing aristocracy is perhaps better termed 'the nobility' – that is, consisting of men, patrician and plebeian, whose families were 'known' (*nobiles*). This, however, did not work to cut the majority of the population out of the political process, since ultimately all those wealthy nobles who sought office were subject to the popular will.

As we have seen, Polybius admired the republic's government because of the fact that it brought together elements of what Greeks recognised as three different types of constitution – monarchy, aristocracy and democracy. However, whereas the Greek city-states had regularly seen the demise of these because of their exclusiveness, the Roman republic prospered not only because it enjoyed elements of all three but also, importantly, because the three were genuinely interlocked with each other through powers and checks, which precluded the dominance of any one of them.

The Roman republic had no *written* constitution; rather, its practices for government evolved over the centuries. The importance of evolution over revolution was seen as the root of the republic's stability. In the republic's 'mixed constitution' the monarchic element was represented by the magistracy (principally the consulship), the aristocratic by the senate, and the democratic by the assemblies of the whole people (*comitia*) and of the plebeians (*concilium plebis*).

The 'balance' between these elements has received different interpretations over the years; some have accepted that there was a genuine reality to the checks and balances that Polybius noted, whilst others have downgraded, even written off altogether, the notion of a popular role in the process of government. It is true that the institution of patronage must have had some effect on voting-habits, especially before the gradual introduction during the second century of secret balloting in assembly-voting. Patronage was a traditional 'institution' in Rome, by which the rich and influential provided help and advice of varying kinds to those less fortunate; patrons expected loyalty (*fides*), at least, in return. Although it may be possible to overplay the role of patronage in political life, the obligations it placed upon those involved were real enough.

Further, as we shall see, the organisation of voting in the assemblies did not follow the principle of 'one man, one vote'; in the most weighty of the popular assemblies, the *comitia centuriata*, the wealthy had a clear edge in 'voting-power' over those less fortunate. Similarly, the fact that, as we have seen, the tenure of the magistracies and the membership of the senate were unsalaried clearly meant that in practice they were open only to those of means. Again, whilst the popular assemblies had to be summoned to meet (by a magistrate), the senate could meet at will. Respect for tradition (*mos maiorum*) will also have ensured that the members of the nobility were generally respected as men of experience and breeding, tried and tested over the years and thus the source of accumulated wisdom on matters political, military, religious and legal. As we shall see in Chapter 3, it was also of relevance to any discussion of popular power that Rome was frequently at war during the period of the republic, and that as Roman territory and, with it, citizenship expanded, many voters will have lived further away from Rome itself, the place where, of course, votes were cast.

However, despite these considerations, it remains clear that the people were important and had weight: tradition, for example, shows how, during the 'Struggle of the Orders', popular pressure was exerted by threats with a more modern 'ring' to them; namely, withdrawal of co-operation, especially in the military context. Even if such episodes did not occur precisely in the way that Roman historians recorded, the point itself remains valid. Again, political oratory was a major feature of Roman life: would this have been the case if the intended audience, the Roman people, were mere spectators of and ciphers in the political process itself? Further, it has to be kept in mind that formal voting in the popular assemblies was preceded over a period by a series of four informal meetings (*contiones*) at which the matters which were at issue and which would eventually come to a vote were rehearsed before the people or plebeians. This does not suggest that, in the Roman republic, the people should be dismissed as of little or no account in the political process.

We shall now turn individually to the three principal elements in the 'Polybian balance' – the magistrates, the senate and the people's assemblies:

## THE MAGISTRATES

*(The duties of the magistrates in the Roman republic are laid out more fully in Appendix II.)*

It is thought by some that the magistracy had its origins in the regal period in the form of men who led the kings' armies into battle: these magistrates *may* at that stage have been called *praetors*: *prae-itor* is one who 'goes in front'. Traditionally, the office of consul emerged in 509 BC with the birth of the republic; however, it has been suggested that, whilst 509 may have been significant as the year in which the great Temple of Jupiter on the Capitoline Hill was dedicated, the republic itself did not come into being for another half-century or so. It seems likely that, politically and militarily, the early-fifth century was a turbulent period in central Italy, when control of the site of Rome may have been a matter of envious dispute amongst local 'warlords'; some hint of this is provided in the 'heroic' stories narrated in the second book of the Augustan historian, Livy.

The founding of the republic and the dedication of the temple may have been brought together in the tradition in order to associate this temple closely with the republic rather than with the kings. If, however, the republic is to be 're-dated' to *c.* 460, then the consuls would appear to have antedated it. The inception of consuls in Rome may indeed mark a change in political emphasis, as the name means 'one who *consults*'.

If the consulship represents the 'residue' of regal power, then great care was taken to ensure that the consuls were kept under control and could not easily move to establish a kingship (*regnum*). First, two were elected to hold office for a year; after that time they handed their power over and were required formally to account for their tenures of office.

In the dual magistracy, the man who said 'no' prevailed over his colleague in the event of disagreement between them: the dual office may also have had practical reasons behind it; it has been suggested that one consul may have led armies whilst his colleague headed up the administration in Rome, and that they may have alternated, possibly on a monthly basis. Consuls were expected to consult their peers in the senate and the people to secure the decision-making process.

As the Roman republic grew in size and complexity, so the burden on the consuls must have become increasingly intolerable. To deal with this, new offices were created to handle specific areas of administration: quaestors, for example, aided the consuls in the financial side of their responsibilities, whilst the censorship was created in order to relieve the consuls of such duties as their care for the republic's 'moral fabric' and supervision of the senate's membership. Censors also came to 'assess' the Roman people for 'taxation', which meant placing them into a property group (*classis*), which determined the level of their contribution in time of war and, related to that, their place in the organisation of the *comitia centuriata*, the assembly which has been dubbed 'the nation at arms'.

Praetors were 'brought back' in the mid-fourth century: ostensibly this provided men whose duties lay principally in the legal field, such as the *praetor peregrinus* who dealt with the interaction between citizens and non-citizens. Praetors could also deputise for or 'supplement' the consuls, particularly in the area of military command. Some, however, have argued that the decision to 'recreate' what was at first an exclusively patrician office came at a

time (367 BC) when it was enacted that one of the annual consulships should be reserved for plebeians. Both consuls and praetors
were invested with 'military authority' (*imperium*), which was
conferred upon them by the longest-surviving of the popular
assemblies, the *comitia curiata*, after their election to office in
another body.

Gradually, over the years, the 'rules of tenure' of these offices
became more closely organised and regulated, so that an order of
tenure came into being, together with recognised minimum ages
of tenure, intervals between offices and between successive tenures
of the same office. This organisation of offices was called the *cursus
honorum*; rising through it to the consulship was a man's *dignitas*
and, by doing this, he demonstrated himself as worthy of his
ancestors and as enhancing his family's standing. For members of
the nobility, the ability to progress along the *cursus* represented
freedom from the domination of others – that is, *libertas*. Whilst
there were many laws touching upon the *cursus honorum*, the most
important were the *lex Villia annalis* of 180 BC and a *lex annalis* of
Cornelius Sulla, passed in the late 80s. It is significant that, in his
reconstruction of the republic after the battle of Actium in 31 BC,
the emperor Augustus retained the *cursus honorum*, but ensured
that it came to serve the needs of the republic and empire rather
than those of individuals.

In times of emergency there was provision for the election of a
*dictator*, if both of the consuls agreed to this course of action. Such
was the ingrained fear of monarchy, however, that dictatorships
were held in not more than two six-month spells. Such 'regular'
dictatorships were, of course, of a different order from the
extended tenures later held by Julius Caesar in the 40s. Dictators
overrode all of the state's officers and enjoyed immunity from the
exercise of the tribunes' veto – the only office so 'privileged'.

The office of tribune of the plebeians was, according to tradition,
first established in 494 BC. The 'tribal leader' was the plebeians'
own officer; as he was elected by the plebeian citizens alone, his
office was not *de iure* regarded as a magistracy of the republic,
although over the years it came increasingly to be treated as if
effectively it was. The office, of which there were originally two
annual holders (eventually rising to ten), represented leadership of
the plebeians in the practical sense of presiding over meetings of

the plebeian assembly (*concilium plebis*), although its real 'teeth' rested in its power of veto.

Originally, the tribunes 'interceded' physically between a plebeian and a magistrate in order to protect the former; eventually, this process of intercession was enhanced into the ability to stop a piece of legislation or to halt public business by declaring a veto (*intercessio*). This ability placed considerable power into the hands of holders of the office and made them great assets to the political groups/factions (*partes*) in the senate and assemblies. In the early republic, however, tribunes, as non-magistrates, were not even members of the senate, but sat on a bench in the senate's doorway so that they could monitor proceedings. The tribunes had one further major 'asset' – the sacrosanctity of their persons: if a tribune's veto were set aside or if he was otherwise illegally handled, the plebeian section of the community was under religious obligation to avenge its wronged tribune.

These, then, were the offices (apart from the tribunate) which constituted the executive arm of the republic's government, but which exercised their roles in consultation with the senate and the assemblies. It was said that the magistrates were motivated by patriotism and family glory (*patria et gloria*): many of the problems of the later years of the republic were caused by their paying an ever-greater heed to the latter and correspondingly less to the former. This state of affairs and the necessity of its correction by the emperor, Augustus, was a principal theme of the *Roman Odes* (*Odes* III.1–6) of the Augustan poet, Horace.

## THE SENATE

The senate went back to the regal period of Rome's history, when the heads of aristocratic households (*patres*) were used by the kings as their advisers. Officially, in those days, the senate had 'teeth' only in the period of *interregnum* between kings: it was evidently the senators who arranged the passage of power from a dead king to his successor.

Once the republic had been established, the senate assumed a stronger and wider role, perhaps principally because of the accumulated wisdom in the major areas of government, foreign affairs, finance, law and religion that was thought to be represented

by senators and past generations of their families. It is little
wonder that Pyrrhus, the king of the Greek state of Epirus, in the
early-third century BC, referred to the senate as an 'assembly of
kings'; or that Marcus Cicero, in the first century BC, described
the magistrates as the senate's 'servants'. Many, indeed, have seen
the senate as the body which gave the Roman republic the stability and continuity of government that characterised it until the
second century BC.

The senate was elected by no one: its membership was overseen
initially by the consuls, but later by the censors. These men, who
were former consuls, were thought to have sufficient standing
(*auctoritas*) to avoid the exertion upon them of undue influence.
The criteria which they employed with regard to the senate were
to ensure that all former magistrates had a place on the senate's
roll, but that those men who were regarded as unworthy of the
honour because of character or conduct should be excluded.

The senate met as it wished, and it did not need to be specific-
ally convened, although it did meet to be consulted by a magistrate. On these occasions, although the magistrate could curtail
discussion when he thought that he had heard sufficient 'advice',
such discussion took place according to rank amongst the senate's
members. In the late republic – and our best evidence comes from
Sallust's account of the famous debate on the fates of the appre-
hended Catilinarians in 63 BC – the first to speak in answer to
the presiding officer were former consuls (*consulares*), although if
the debate were taking place later in the year than the annual
elections for the following year's magistrates (in the late republic,
usually held in June), the consuls-designate took precedence over
the ex-consuls in the giving of their opinions. These were then
followed by the praetorian and tribunician groups. On most occasions, the number of views heard might be quite small, although
in the Catilinarian debate the presiding consul (Marcus Cicero)
continued to take views until he reached the tribunes-designate –
and, in particular, Marcus Cato; this was to ensure that the last
voice that senators heard before voting was a ringing endorsement
of the consul's own hard line. Junior senators rarely, if ever, spoke,
and were called *pedarii* ('walkers'), meaning that their function
was to walk to the place of voting.

The result of the vote was the passing of a decree (*senatus consultum*) encapsulating the senate's view; although very influential, this was not binding unless passed into law by a popular assembly. Magistrates and tribunes were not bound to consult the senate in this way, although after the passing of the Publilian laws of 339 BC and the Hortensian law of 287 they seldom omitted to do so in practice. It is little wonder that in such a climate Cicero held the view that he did concerning the relationship between senate and magistrates; further, it may seem strange that he thought of the magistrates as the servants of the senate, despite the fact that those magistrates had been elected to their offices *by the people*.

One particular decree had an especially emotive role – the *senatus consultum ultimum* (a decree of 'national emergency'). Under it the consuls were advised to use the coercive powers in their *imperium* to deal with men who were seen or were claimed to be 'enemies of the republic'. The legal status of such a decree was questionable: the people as the ultimate source of rights were legally alone in being able to remove them. Thus, as was pointed out more than once, magistrates who acted on the basis of an 'ultimate decree' to banish or even execute somebody were running a considerable personal risk.

In practice, for many centuries the standing of the senate and of its individual members, reinforced by the influence of their patronage, was sufficient to leave the senate as the *de facto* government of the republic. This state of affairs was probably the real source of stability. In addition, the senate assumed the right of control over foreign affairs and, after the abolition of direct taxation on citizens in Italy in 167, over financial matters also. The people were generally not in a position to defy the combination of senate and magistrates and, in any case, had to appreciate that, when they were 'called up' for military service, their officers (the incumbent magistrates) enjoyed the power of life and death over them, until the early-second century. The operation of this power could not be appealed under the citizen's right of *provocatio*, until (evidently in the early-second century) the latter was extended onto the battlefield; even then, discipline remained harsh, and the practice of decimation survived.

It was with the ending of this state of affairs and the introduction of secret balloting in the assemblies, as well as a developing awareness on the people's part of state affairs and how they were affected by them, that the people's acquiescence came to be taken less for granted, with consequently a growing need to persuade people through oratory of a course of action that was to be taken.

A greater sense of individualism amongst senators and a feeling that they were 'playing' for ever-higher stakes – especially when from the late-second century BC the army itself was more readily available as part of the political armoury – ensured that the senate's dominance came under increasing pressure. Thus, the republic's stability began to break down, culminating in the anarchy and civil strife which characterised its final decades.

## THE PEOPLE'S ASSEMBLIES

*(The make-up, duties and procedures of the republic's popular assemblies are laid out in Appendix III.)*

It may appear strange that the Roman republic maintained four different popular assemblies – three of the whole citizen-body (*populus*) and one of the plebeian citizens alone. The three assemblies of the *populus* were the *comitia curiata, comitia centuriata* and *comitia tributa*; the plebeian assembly was called the *concilium plebis*. These assemblies, between them, handled electoral, governmental and judicial business, although during the last two centuries of the republic their judicial functions increasingly passed to 'specialist courts' (*quaestiones*) over which praetors presided.

These assemblies had come into being at different times, for different purposes and responding to different conditions. The oldest of them was the *comitia curiata* (assembly of the *curiae*); the thirty *curiae* were the districts of Rome in the regal period. In historical times, this body was superseded by other assemblies, and the full assembly of the *comitia curiata* was replaced by thirty representative lictors. Although the *comitia curiata* lost its main functions and remained in the system as a kind of 'fossil', it continued to handle such matters as the validation of wills, the confirming of adoptions and the formal conferring of *imperium* on senior magistrates elected to office in other bodies. Occasionally, however, circumstances might bring it into the foreground, as when, in 59, it approved the transference by adoption of Publius Clodius into a plebeian family to facilitate his campaign for election to the tribunate of the plebeians; or again, when in 54 it refused to confer *imperium* on to Clodius' brother, Appius Claudius, although he had been properly elected to a consulship.

In terms of its business, the *comitia centuriata* was clearly the most important of the Roman assemblies; traditionally, it had come into being in the late regal period and, as its name suggests, it reflected the preoccupation of the citizen-body with preparation for warfare. As such, it provides a good illustration of the principle that those who contributed most to the Roman state should expect to reap the greatest privileges. In its organisation into *classes* and *centuriae*, it quite openly gave most opportunity to influence events to the wealthiest of the citizens, who between them were allocated a majority of the voting centuries; on the other hand, the poorest of the citizens were placed in large numbers in a very small number of *centuriae*. The point was made the more sharply because voting stopped once a majority of the 193 centuries had been reached, each century counting for one vote. It is not surprising that Marcus Cicero should have referred to this body as his 'army of wealthy men'; it was a body that was most obviously 'in tune' with the views of those who tended to occupy the magistracies and to enjoy membership of the senate.

The *comitia tributa* (or 'assembly of the tribes') may have come into being at around the time of the establishment of the *comitia centuriata*, for it reflected a change from the three so-called 'Romulean' tribes to a larger number which may have been part of the same reforms which have traditionally been attributed to the penultimate king, Servius Tullius. It is uncertain how many tribes were established in the first instance; eventually, however, there were thirty-five, of which thirty-one were 'rural' and four 'urban'; undoubtedly, the thirty-five voting units of this assembly were far easier to manage than the 193 centuries of the *comitia centuriata* and, probably because of this, the *comitia tributa* came to deal with an increasing volume of public business. Although originally allocation to tribes was evidently done on a geographical basis, the spread of Roman citizenship over the years meant that allocation became more arbitrary and thus, in a real sense, the assembly became more democratic.

Nonetheless, this assembly, too, had drawbacks: in the first place, those allocated to rural tribes were country dwellers, and only the more wealthy of these will have been able to make the journey to Rome to vote. In time, when some country dwellers had come to settle in Rome, the fact that they remained as voters in their rural tribes meant that the assembly came increasingly to reflect the views of the urban population. In fact, whilst we might regard the *comitia tributa* as less undemocratic than the *comitia centuriata*, it was no more representative.

The fourth assembly did not represent the whole people, only the plebeian section of it: the *concilium plebis* had come into being as a result of plebeian agitation during the early part of the 'Struggle of the Orders'. It met under the presidency of the 'tribal leaders' of the plebeians (that is, the tribunes), but initially could take decisions that affected the plebeians alone; these decisions (*plebiscita*) could, however, subsequently be 'adopted' by a magistrate and taken through the senate and *populus* to become law. The organisation of the *concilium plebis* was based on the thirty-five tribes, although of course lacking the patrician citizens, and its procedures were similar. In fact, the tendency of Roman authors to use the term, 'the Tribes', indiscriminately for the *comitia tributa* and for the *concilium plebis* sometimes makes it difficult for us to determine which assembly is meant.

One of the final areas of agitation of the 'Struggle of the Orders' concerned the status of the *concilium plebis* and of its decisions. A law passed in 339 by Publilius Philo and evidently re-enacted half-a-century later (287) in the *lex Hortensia* confirmed that the decisions of the *concilium plebis* (*plebiscita*) should be regarded as laws binding the whole people: the Assembly of the Plebeians had thus become a sovereign body. What difference, then, did this concession make to the government of the republic? In the first place, it must be borne in mind that earlier concessions, which had opened up the senate and the magistracies to plebeian membership, made the decisions of 339 and 287 far less dramatic in effect than they might seem; earlier changes had opened up participation in government to plebeians, although in practice only those who could afford to participate will have been able to take advantage of the changing situation. In effect, this meant that the wealthier plebeians were already identifying their interests with those of the patricians, not only making them less likely to wish to disturb the *status quo* but also in the process effectively removing from the plebeians their natural leaders. In other words, there was little chance that the *concilium plebis* would become a 'hotbed of discontent': the concession to it of sovereignty was thus perfectly safe.

Second, as we shall see, an effect of the growth of Roman influence outside the city itself had been to open up opportunities for wealth creation and for the fulfilment of ambitions on a scale not previously contemplated; the nobility – patrician and plebeian – was probably as a result more concerned that threats to its corporate supremacy would emerge from its own ranks than from, for example, the urban plebeians. Thus, as the concession of sovereignty was granted to the plebeians, so there was a recognition that magistrates should as a matter of course 'consult with' the senate prior to 'going to' the people. In this way, the nobility was able, for a time at least, to exercise some measure of control over those whom it was coming to fear most (see Figure 1).

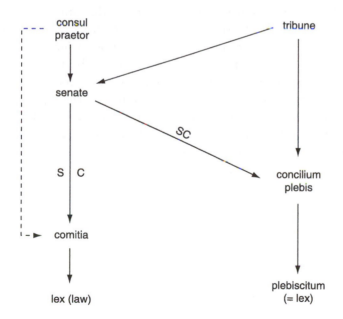

*Figure 1* Legislation in Rome after 287 BC
Note: SC = *Senatus Consulto* (by decree of the senate)

It is also important to remember that the procedures of the assemblies made them more manageable than might otherwise have been the case; nor was this attributable simply to the practice of group voting. As we have seen, the consultation of the people by a magistrate was not a simple process, but consisted of four 'informal' meetings (*contiones*) on separate occasions, the fourth being followed immediately by the formal reconstitution of the meeting concerned into a *voting* assembly. As a result, apart from voting itself, the people's part was passive: they listened to the magistrate explaining his proposition and to those whom the magistrate invited to speak. There were no questions or amendments from the floor, and no general discussion of the matter concerned; after all, this had already been discussed in the senate. This does not, however, mean that the magistrate concerned could afford to ignore the popular interest; he still had to win his vote, and so needed the full benefit of his skills of persuasion. Not only this, however, but he could never forget that it would probably be only a short time before he would be back before these same people seeking election to a further office.

Thus, in the Roman republic, although the formal protection of democracy might sometimes appear to have been less than adequate, there were practical considerations which served its interests. The undermining of the republic's stability came not so much from a dissatisfied democratic pressure-group as from a collection of pressures which were exerted on the republic as a result of the physical growth of Rome's interests in Italy and beyond. To the expansion of the empire, why it occurred and what effects it had we shall now turn.

# 2

## THE GROWTH OF EMPIRE

As we have seen, the growth of the Roman empire has been held by many to have been the 'overarching' cause of the breakdown of the 'old republic'. It is important, therefore, to explore in greater detail the nature of that growth and of the stresses that developed as a result of territorial expansion both in Italy and on a wider canvas. (For a list of provinces of the Roman empire, see Appendix IV.)

The earliest expansion, not surprisingly, took place within Rome's immediate neighbourhood as the early republic needed to acquire more land for its citizens and to 'put space' between itself and its enemies. Such motives remained powerful until the middle years of the third century BC, by which time Rome either exercised some kind of control or enjoyed influence over most of Italy south of the river Po. There were undoubtedly other motives, also. For example, it was obviously in Rome's interest to be seen to be supporting friends and allies, as when she became involved in conflicts in southern Italy in the fourth and third centuries BC which did not, initially at least, affect her directly. Beyond this, there were 'pre-emptive strikes' and punitive activities, not to mention the desire on the part of her aristocratic leaders to acquire booty, power and reputation, all of which were the fuel of election campaigns. It would, however, be premature to formalise such relationships as Rome had with Italian communities as constituting an 'Italian Confederacy' until the very late years of the republic in the first century BC.

Initially, Rome was apparently working together with the other people of the surrounding neighbourhood, Latium, to secure the area against tribal enemies, who probably realised as sharply as did the Romans how important control of the lower Tiber valley was. The site of Rome itself commanded freedom of movement in the valley and, in particular, access to the salt supplies of the river's estuary, which were to be secured, probably in the early-fourth century, by the foundation of a *colonia* at Ostia, which tradition held to have been Rome's earliest such foundation. However, by the close of the fifth century BC, her attention was moving more to the north, towards Etruscan city-states such as Veii which was captured in 390 after a century of intermittent warfare; indeed, it is held by some that Lars Porsenna was a ruler at Veii, and that his intervention in Rome in the fifth century, recorded by Livy, should be seen as part of this rivalry. The land and people of Veii were made part of the Roman state. Almost immediately, Rome was threatened by an enemy from rather further to the north – Gauls from beyond the river Po. The sacking of Rome in 390 by these people was thereafter held to be one of the major formative influences on Roman attitudes to the outside world; certainly, it prompted the building of defensive structures in Rome – the so-called 'Servian Walls'.

From that point the speed of Roman progress in Italy quickened, and with it came a rather more hard-headed attitude towards political and social relationships with Italian communities. During the fourth century, Rome turned her attention to the south – to the people (and land) of Campania and to the Samnites, a hill-people of central southern Italy, who were causing disturbance to both the Campanians and many of the Greek city-states, such as Naples (*Neapolis*), which had been established in the coastal regions. A major result of this was a gain of land of high agricultural quality, together with a decision to change the Latin League, previously consisting of nominally equal partners, to an organisation which acknowledged Roman hegemony.

With this growth of territory, the time had evidently come by the second half of the fourth century to bring some shape to the 'legal' side of Rome's relationships with Italian communities:

some were simply absorbed into the Roman state, their citizens becoming full Roman citizens. Whilst this might be seen as a particularly sensible and generous move (as it was later represented by the emperor Claudius), it has to be remembered that many of the new citizens would not be able to afford the time to come to Rome to vote, nor would most of them command the wealth to be able even to contemplate attempting to win office.

Others lost certain special privileges that they may have enjoyed or, whilst remaining allies of Rome, had to defer to her in matters of foreign policy; these retained 'Latin rights' such as *coniubium* (right of intermarriage) and *commercium* (right of enforcing contracts through each other's legal mechanisms). They also had the right to 'migrate' to each other's territory and assume citizenship there. For peoples new to a relationship with Rome a fresh system was devised, known as *Civitas sine suffragio* – that is, holding *coniubium* and *commercium*, though without the political rights of Roman citizenship, such as voting and holding office.

In the 'conquest' of Italy, some land was left with its original owners, but much became the property of Rome (*ager publicus/* 'public land'), and was available to be leased to locals, to be used for agricultural settlement by Roman citizens or for the establishment of towns (*coloniae*) which were populated by groups of citizens sent from Rome or from Latin allies. Besides this, some communities were offered treaties, the terms of which varied in implication from alliances to virtual dependency. These conquests also provided a basis for Rome's future military success, in terms both of large supplies of manpower and access to a variety of military tactics. In the Roman army from this point, Roman citizens made up the legions, whilst the Italian allies (*socii*) were arranged in smaller contingents; eligibility for military service was assessed on the basis of property, and since most property consisted of land, the bulk of the burden of service consequently fell on to the shoulders of farmers. This was to cause problems in the future.

Such a network of relationships effectively guaranteed Roman domination in central Italy; this proved to be the springboard for the completion, by the early third century, of the conquest of Etruscan city-states and the Gauls of the north and the Samnites of the south, the latter despite Rome's suffering one of

her most humiliating military defeats in 321 at the Caudine
Forks. Her military successes were followed up by an expansion of
the political arrangements already described, and by a programme
of construction in Italy of a network of major roads.

It was her involvement in the south of Italy which led to her
much wider Mediterranean role: for conflict with Tarentum
(Taranto) in the early years of the third century prompted the
Tarentines to call for help from Pyrrhus, the king of Epirus in
mainland Greece, who was finally defeated in 275. Very soon
after this, a series of disputes in south-west Italy and Sicily, which
in essence did not directly concern Rome, but in which importantly her help was sought, brought her into conflict with the
great trading power on the southern side of the Mediterranean,
Carthage. From the early-third to the mid-second century Rome
was to be involved in a series of conflicts and 'diplomatic initiatives' with the Carthaginians (the three 'Punic Wars'), and with
states in mainland Greece and the Hellenistic east. These were to
see her grow from an Italian to a 'world'-power, with major consequences for her political, military, social, economic and cultural
fabric.

Three wars were fought against Carthage (264–241; 218–202;
149–146); although this is not the place to recount the courses of
these wars in detail, some consequences should be highlighted. It
should be said at the outset that Carthage was not the overween-
ing and aggressive military power depicted in Roman propaganda; the chief interest of the North African city was to advance
her trading and commercial activities which were based largely
upon her extraordinarily rich agricultural hinterland. It is not
surprising that in time (by the third century AD) the North African
provinces were amongst the wealthiest of the Roman empire. For
the Carthaginians in the third century BC wars were sometimes
necessary to strengthen economic dominance and to achieve new
markets; it is worth noting, however, that Carthage did not maintain a standing army but rather recruited mercenaries (mostly
from Greek states) when required.

In the prelude to the first Punic War, the Carthaginians who
had already established a 'market-dominance' in Sicily were seeking to extend this on to the Italian mainland; in the course of the
war, the Romans not only established themselves, of necessity, as a

naval power, building their own vessels after the Carthaginian model instead of relying on Greek allies, but also came to appreciate that their system of annual magistracies, whilst suitable for campaigning on a seasonal basis, was inadequate for the conduct of extended warfare. Thus, the lengthening of a magistrate's tenure by making him a promagistrate (proconsul; propraetor), which had already been done on a very small scale in the late fourth century, was now put to greater use in order to ensure some continuity of command. Such extensions of authority were evidently not seen as a threat to the political equilibrium as they remained completely at the discretion of the senate. To maintain the Roman grip on Italy, the 'programme' of *colonia* foundation continued through the war and afterwards, although it came to a virtual halt in the later years of the third century. Finally, Rome's victory at the end of this released the Carthaginian hold on Sicily which, in 241, became the first overseas province of the Roman empire.

In the wake of the war, the Romans were harsh: so great was the financial indemnity placed upon Carthage that she could not even afford to pay off the soldiers who had fought for her. This itself led to disturbances, out of which eventually Rome gained control of two further 'offshore' islands, Sardinia and Corsica, which, like Sicily, became provinces. Rome also clearly demonstrated her attitude to disloyalty on the part of her Italian neighbours: the Faliscans, to the north of Rome, revolted in the very moment of Rome's victory in Sicily. The punishment was severe: the complete destruction of their chief town, *Falerii Veteres* (Civitacastellana), and its replacement by a new town in a less defensible position (*Falerii Novi*: S Maria di Falerii Novi). A further effect of the war was the Roman decision to issue coinage, silver and lighter bronze; the purpose of this was probably to release more bronze for the manufacture of weapons, as well as paying suppliers; the new coinage, much of which was probably initially made for Rome by Greek city-states in southern Italy, was also of course far more convenient than the old bronze bars for the conduct of commerce.

The second Punic War was in many ways a consequence of the first: the loss of the Sicilian markets was, for Carthage, so serious a matter that Hamilcar Barca was sent in search of new markets in

Spain. It is likely also that his aristocratic colleagues in Carthage were pleased to be able to put some distance between themselves and Hamilcar, not least because of his excessively hostile attitude to Rome over the severity of the post-war settlement. Hamilcar took with him his young son, Hannibal, who inherited from his father his anti-Roman obsession. It became Hannibal's 'mission' to use Spain as a training-ground for an army which could take the Romans on and avenge the earlier defeat. His and Carthage's refusal to accede to Roman demands led to the outbreak of the second war in 218.

This war was of great importance for its effects: Hannibal's crossing of the Alps and his apparently unstoppable progress through northern Italy certainly led to agricultural distress and enhanced longer-term fears of invasion, although his much-fabled use of elephants probably caused as many problems for his own army as for that of his opponents. It is likely, too, that Rome's attitude to her Italian allies was hardened by the decision of some of them, more from exhaustion than conviction, to throw in their lot with Hannibal. The Carthaginian's great error, however, was his decision to ignore Rome itself and head south in order to detach as many of Rome's allies as possible. Whilst this achieved some success, a growing problem for Hannibal was his difficulty in gaining reinforcements; his hopes of these coming from Spain were dashed by the activities of a Roman army in Spain under Publius Cornelius Scipio (later 'Africanus'), who had been working to achieve an army as efficient and personally devoted to their commander as that of Hannibal had been; further, Carthaginian hopes of receiving help from Philip V of Macedon came to nothing. In reality, the tide had now turned: Scipio (elected consul for 205) was permitted to take a force across the Mediterranean to Africa where, at Zama (in modern Tunisia) in 202, Hannibal was finally defeated. Again, the terms imposed on Carthage were severe, and in the aftermath Rome added to her overseas empire two new provinces in Spain (Tarraconensis and Baetica).

Rome had survived her toughest military and political test and had won a victory which, in the view of the historian, Polybius, opened up the prospect of world domination: the Roman political machine had held firm with the senate at the helm; so, too, had the people and, in the main, the 'Italian alliance'. It may be that it was the confidence born of this success that led so rapidly to a decision to launch a war into Greece; this may have begun as the punishment of Philip V for his past involvement with Hannibal, but it might also be regarded as a 'pre-emptive strike' in defence of Rome's regional friends (such as the island of Rhodes and the kings of Egypt and Pergamum). It was to result, by the middle of the second century BC, in the tying of large parts of the eastern Mediterranean into the Roman imperial machine. For some time Rome tried to secure arrangements with various Greek states which would leave their administration in the hands of pro-Roman groups; generally, and not surprisingly, she dealt more easily with oligarchies than with democracies. On the whole, however, the local arrangements that were set up in various places tended to lack stability, leading to the need for further military involvement after a time. This was bound to put a strain on Rome's military resources.

It may be that it was the continuing failure to find lasting solutions to government in the Greek east and a fear of a resurgence of the power of Carthage that, in 146, brought about two acts that have been regarded as clear signals of a hardening attitude in Rome to relations with other states: the complete destruction of Carthage, which brought to an end the third Punic War, coincided with a similar treatment of the Greek city of Corinth; both Carthage and northern Greece were reorganised as provinces (respectively Africa and Macedonia). Not unreasonably, many have taken 146 as marking a turning point in Rome's progress from a small city-state to an imperialistic power; we shall now turn, therefore, to the effects on Rome and her people of the century of warfare and imperial growth that had elapsed since the outbreak of the first war against Carthage in 264 BC.

As we have seen, in the wake of the 'Struggle of the Orders' the third century had brought about changes in Rome: the quality of life for ordinary people had benefited from the influx of wealth and goods which were the prizes of victory in war; at the same time, the government of Rome had broadened as the wealthier plebeians were able to identify their interests more closely with those of the patricians. Possibly, near-continuous warfare removed both the incentive and the opportunity for political 'boat-rocking'; after all, the republic appeared to be prospering under an aristocratic government which resided largely in the senate's hands.

However, imperial growth brought changes both for society and for individuals: for some it was possible to contemplate a lifestyle that was far more luxurious than before, and this unsurprisingly led to attempts to curb it through sumptuary legislation, much of which was probably the subject of mockery rather than of compliance. The second century saw the beginnings of a shift from simple methods of construction in both public and domestic architecture to those that were more grandiose – the copying of Greek styles, the introduction of the use of marble and the first use of concrete as a medium for construction. This will have caused disquiet amongst traditionalists, a disquiet that persisted in certain quarters, as we see two and three centuries later in the writings of Horace and Juvenal; the complaint uttered in Juvenal's third satire – 'I hate this Greek city of ours' – could well have been on the lips of some in the second century BC.

So building changed, as did religion and writing: new cults inevitably found their way to Italy in the aftermath of warfare; some of these were 'Romanised' and accepted, whilst others, such as the orgies associated with Bacchus (Dionysus), were effectively outlawed as 'morally subversive', as we see in a surviving edict of 186 BC. Successful warfare brought prisoners-of-war, who were then sold in the slave markets. Those who were Greek and educated might very often find themselves taken on as tutors and 'secretaries' in the houses of the aristocracy. In those roles they could introduce a taste of a different culture, bringing Greek style and content to traditional types of writing; for many there was nothing wrong with this as it opened new horizons. Indeed, 'budding' Roman authors were advised to study their Greek originals 'by night and day'. Over time, the development of this Graeco-Roman culture was seen as a great benefit, and it was effectively enshrined in the Augustan revolution of the late-first century BC.

Immediately, however, the effects of warfare and imperial growth brought problems as well as opportunities: the Roman army was traditionally one of peasants (*assidui*) whose landholding formed their qualification for service. In the early days, when the bulk of fighting was in Italy, it was conducted on a seasonal basis, and farmers could generally manage to combine both military service and agriculture. Traditionalists approved of this, because it was reckoned that those who 'got their hands dirty' in Italy's soil would have a greater commitment to defending the homeland; the 'romantic idyll' of the bucolic life undoubtedly had something to do with this. It is not likely that, with the growth of empire and, therefore, of wars fought at a greater distance from home, men were called upon to serve more campaigns, but the campaigns in which they did fight disrupted their lives more seriously, making it harder for them to support home and family. Indeed, this problem may have been exacerbated by the importation of cheap grain from abroad, making it harder for small farmers to compete, especially in the hinterland of the ports. This will obviously have become a problem around Rome itself.

Contemporaneously with this, the influx of money into the hands of the wealthy allowed those who were looking for a sound investment opportunity to purchase land that was left vacant by farmer-soldiers. Further, the booming slave market provided plenty of cheap labour. Thus, in some parts of Italy at least, the influx of money and slaves led to a displacement of free labour from the land and the growth of large estates (*latifundia*), which were able to conduct their activities in a far more organised and effective manner. How much difficulty was brought to military recruitment by this is unclear, although there is some evidence in the mid-second century in the form of resistance to the military levy. This will have been the origin of the so-called 'land problem' which was rearing its head in the second half of the second century.

The aristocracy found their ambitions fuelled by the new opportunities: leading armies to victory brought fame to a man and his family; it was a means by which he could show himself to be mindful of the customs of his ancestors (*mos maiorum*). Cicero was later to say that *military* glory outstripped all other types. In this way, the aristocrat could envisage becoming ever-wealthier, and his money could be put to good use in socially beneficent activities, such as the provision of public buildings which both gave work and represented useful facilities. The families of Aemilius Paullus, of Cato the Censor and of Tiberius Sempronius Gracchus all put up the money in the second century for the construction of public halls (respectively the *Basilica Aemilia, Basilica Porcia, Basilica Sempronia*) around the Forum in Rome. Wealth, clientage, military glory and public munificence were all components of *auctoritas* (prestige) which led both to the winning of office and to respect for one's views.

Imperial growth brought problems for Rome itself: in addition to the consequences of the trends noted above, Rome found herself having to develop ways of governing the lands which she was acquiring and making into provinces. Although the first province (Sicily) was governed by electing an additional annual praetor in Rome, there was no great enthusiasm for an open-ended enlargement of the power base. In other words, it was not regarded as satisfactory to elect an extra official each time a new province was created. The 'solution' was an extension of the use of promagistracies, the practice already brought into play in the third century to deal with the need for some continuity in military commands. Thus, provinces were to be governed by proconsuls and propraetors, men who had already won and served a consulship/ praetorship in Rome and who would proceed afterwards to govern a province for a year. The pitfalls of this became more obvious with time: for some saw their provincial terms as opportunities for pillage, either of works of art or money, which would either pay off debts incurred in the last election campaign or 'prime the pumps' for the next one. There was a court in which extortionate officials could be tried (*Quaestio de rebus repetundis*); however, it was virtually impossible for wronged provincials to bring prosecutions without first obtaining the services of a Roman patron, and well-nigh impossible to persuade a jury composed of the defendant's peers, many of whom will have been as guilty as him in the past or who would expect to be in the future. It was, as we shall see in Chapter 3, part of the legislative programme of Gaius Gracchus to make important changes in the procedures of this court.

Finally, there were tax systems to be introduced in the provinces and taxes to be collected – direct taxes on property and indirect on the movement of produce. In some places, these could be collected through existing urban agencies; there was, however, no appropriate 'civil service' in the Roman system, and so taxes were generally collected by 'auctioning' them in Rome, where the right to collect would be bought by groups of wealthy men (*societates publicanorum*), consisting usually of members of the equestrian order (Rome's wealthiest men, second only to senators). In this way, taxes were assessed not according to people's ability to pay, but according to what the 'market would bear'; those unable to pay would often find their lives made wretched by being forced into the clutches of Roman moneylenders, who could be relied upon to charge extravagant rates of interest. The exploitation of many of the natural resources of the empire was organised in a similar fashion, although in these cases the state had a mechanism for controlling the working and the profits – by limiting the size of work-gangs and the number of days worked.

Thus, the effects of imperial growth on Rome, its government and society were deep and wide-ranging, justifying the perception that, in the mid-second century BC, Rome 'stood at the cross-roads'. As we shall see in the next and ensuing chapters, the old republic showed itself unable to adapt sufficiently to avoid its own demise and replacement by a new monarchy: in terms of Rome's traditions the price of imperial growth was indeed high.

# 3

## THE POLITICAL TEMPERATURE RISES: THE GRACCHI, MARIUS AND SULLA

Rome had come through the difficulties of expansion, but only to be beset in the aftermath by an ever more turbulent political climate at home. Many of the reasons for this lay in the events covered in the previous chapter, but a crucial ingredient was provided by the ambitions and personalities of the politicians who came and went between 140 and 80 BC – for example, the brothers Tiberius and Gaius Sempronius Gracchus, Gaius Marius and Lucius Cornelius Sulla. All were men of very different backgrounds, but all would leave an indelible mark on the final century of the old republic.

It has been traditional to see at the heart of Roman political activity in and out of the senate a network of aristocratic families, forming factions who worked together to secure certain aims. These were never 'political parties' in a modern sense – men linked together by policies which derived from a commonly held philosophy; whilst the vicissitudes of family groupings are not fully understood, it is evident that the 'cement' which appears to have held them together was not particularly strong, and alliances might come and go with succeeding generations of families, only to reappear perhaps at a later date. It may be, therefore, that these apparent groupings were far more tenuous than is sometimes assumed, but perhaps represent occasional alliances in the business of seeking office and position.

In the aftermath of the destruction of Carthage and Corinth, the leading figures in Rome were Publius Cornelius Scipio Aemilianus (also known as 'Africanus', the name inherited from his adoptive grandfather) and Appius Claudius Pulcher; evidently the most immediate problem related to Rome's 'public land' (*ager publicus*), land taken in conquest in Italy and usually sold or leased, but sometimes left for 'common use', though with limits on the amount available to a single individual. The matter of Rome's *ager publicus* is inextricably tied to the career of a plebeian noble, the younger Tiberius Sempronius Gracchus, who was tribune of the plebeians in 133 BC. Through his mother, Cornelia, he was, like Aemilianus, a grandson of the conqueror of Hannibal, although he was married to Claudia, the daughter of Appius Claudius; the fathers of Appius Claudius and of Tiberius Gracchus had been closely associated in their careers in the earlier years of the second century. The importance of the events of 133 to those concerned is confirmed in a startling way by the outbreak of violence which brought Tiberius' tribunate to a bloody end (see Figure 2).

What, then, was at stake? It appears that amounts of the *ager publicus* in common use had been taken and held illegally by wealthy men with money to invest in its agricultural development. An attempt was made in 140 by Gaius Laelius, a friend of Aemilianus, to introduce a land bill into the senate, but it was soon dropped; we may assume opposition from men with vested interests. The next attempt was made by Tiberius Gracchus in 133, supported, it appears, by a powerful group of senators which included Appius Claudius, Gracchus' father-in-law. According to the Greek biographer, Plutarch, Tiberius' motive was his utter despair at witnessing for himself the wretched physical state of the land to the north of Rome and the plight of the peasants; it is probable that he was also concerned by the apparently increasing danger of revolts amongst slaves on large agricultural estates. It is also worth adding that, since 140, Rome had been involved in war in Spain (the Numantine War) which appears to have led to a considerable loss of yeomen-farmers. How serious this loss was is hard to gauge, but the fact that Aemilianus was in charge of the conduct of this war is unlikely to have made him a particularly attractive ally for Gracchus, despite the blood connection between

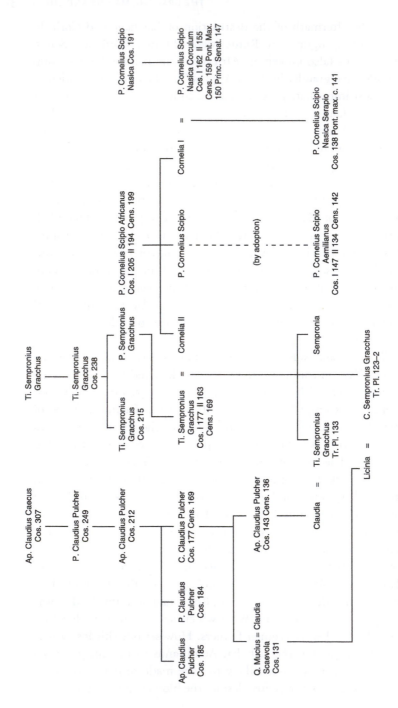

*Figure 2* Stemma showing the links between the Scipiones, Claudii and Sempronii Gracchi in the second century BC

them. It may have been this that led the ambitious Gracchus to seek political support in other quarters.

As far as can be seen, Tiberius' land bill of 133 was similar to that of Laelius seven years earlier, but he had a far greater determination to see it through. Rejected by (or possibly ignoring) the senate, he took the bill, as was possible for a tribune, to the *concilium plebis* – populist politics in action. The bill evidently sought to dispossess landowners of *ager publicus* held above a certain limit, though whether this was a reiteration of an old limit (that is, of 367) or a new one is unclear. The confiscated land was to be redistributed to landless peasants. Undoubtedly, in true demagogic style, the bill's purpose was presented as a measure to rob the rich to give to the poor and perhaps omitting to stress that a resumed landholding would also have placed the obligation of military service on the tenants. The presence in the *concilium plebis* of rich plebeian land-owners will have ensured that opposition would be strong in that body also; indeed, one of Tiberius' fellow tribunes exercised his veto, which Gracchus provocatively set aside: arguing, it would seem, that a tribune who opposed the plebeian will was no 'proper tribune'. Tiberius' action regarding the tribunician veto was, of course, illegal and his threats contrary to religion. His behaviour appears to have become progressively more extreme – a sign of the great importance which he attached to retaining popular support. He proposed that revenue from the kingdom of Pergamum, recently willed to Rome by its late king, Attalus III, should be used to finance his bill, perhaps arguing that a patronal relationship that had existed between his father and Attalus gave him a special privilege in this matter. Finally, Tiberius stood, in clear breach of convention, for a second term as tribune.

This bid for extended power appears to have been the 'last straw' for his opponents, and even some of his original supporters seem by this stage to have been 'lukewarm'; a lynch-mob, headed by the *pontifex maximus*, Publius Cornelius Scipio Nasica (a cousin of Aemilianus), clubbed Tiberius to death in the street and set in motion a witch-hunt against his supporters. Nasica is said to have drawn his toga over his head as he left the senate house; this may have been intended to signify that, as *pontifex maximus*, he was about to conduct sacrifice for the good of the republic. Such, in any case, was probably the gloss which Tiberius' opponents put on what had happened – a man in Rome's senior religious position using religion as a cloak for political gangsterism. In any case, when, later, Aemilianus was asked by a Gracchan supporter, Papirius Carbo, whether it had been right to kill Gracchus, Aemilianus diplomatically responded that it had been if Gracchus had been attempting to establish a *regnum* ('kingship').

Here perhaps we see what was seen as being at stake in these events: the land bill itself was controversial, but not so detested as to lead to its abolition after Gracchus' death. The methods employed by Gracchus, however, were detested; the identity of Gracchus' supporters is probably less important than what the tribune himself did. He rode roughshod through political convention in a thoroughly populist and demagogic way, just the kind of behaviour that, as Aemilianus seemed to suggest, was reminiscent of kings and tyrants. The clue to understanding this episode, therefore, lies in Aemilianus' observation: here is an engaging and significant example of a man who was thought of, in his own time and later, as humane, sophisticated and forward-looking, but who, under extreme political pressure, showed himself to be as thorough a traditionalist as anyone of his class. After all, the continued success of the aristocratic oligarchy was seen as depending upon a continued observance of Rome's long-established traditions. The problem now, however, was that once blood had been shed in pursuance of a political feud, the 'clock could not be turned back'. It was inevitable that, in the post-Gracchan era, it would be easier as a result to settle political issues by resorting to violence: that was the legacy both of Tiberius Gracchus and of the contemporaries who supported and opposed him.

One group of people who had cause for complaint as a result of Tiberius Gracchus' land bill were Rome's Italian allies; in addition to feeling increasingly oppressed by Rome's often high-handed and ungenerous behaviour towards them during the second century, they now found themselves subject to the confiscations of the land bill, but without any form of compensation. The rights and protections of Roman citizenship seemed to them to be the only fair and workable solution to their growing sense of alienation, injustice and inferiority; after all, they shared in the dangers of military and political alliance with Rome, so now they expected fair recompense.

In 125, Marcus Fulvius Flaccus, one of the consuls, proposed that Italians should be asked to choose between Roman citizenship (with its advantages, but also with its consequent loss of local autonomy) and a grant of *provocatio*, which would have provided protection against arbitrary treatment by Roman officials. For some reason, Flaccus' bill did not come to a vote; instead Junius Pennus carried a bill expelling non-Roman Italians from Roman towns. This evidently led to a symbolic, but futile, revolt on the part of the *colonia* of Fregellae (near Monte Cassino), which was put down with the same ruthlessness that Rome had visited upon the Faliscans over a century previously.

Gaius Sempronius Gracchus, the younger brother of the trib-une of 133, now applied himself to the problems of the Italians; becoming tribune for 123, he succeeded in securing election to a second term for 122. The fact that he held office over two years resulted in a great deal of legislation, and it is not always easy to see the chronological relationship between different parts of this, making his motives the more difficult to assess: he may have been intent on seeking revenge for the treatment meted out to his brother, although he is on record as having disapproved of aspects of his brother's tribunate. However, the broad range of his legislation suggests a desire to 'get to grips' with a number of outstanding problems, although his methods display similar populist tendencies to those employed by his brother, legislating through the medium of the *concilium plebis*.

Although the principal areas of his legislation concerned the Italians and the role of the equestrian order, he addressed a number of other contemporary problems, such as stabilising the price of grain that was imported to feed the city populace, and introducing changes in the composition and procedures in the working of the *quaestio de rebus repetundis*, in order to give provincials who had been wronged by Roman officials a better chance of securing justice. He also introduced safeguards, through changes to the law of *provoca-tio*, in an attempt to preclude the kind of political violence that had led to his brother's death: Gracchus made it harder to encompass the death (or other loss of status) on the part of a Roman citizen, and introduced penalties for those who offended. In this, he was of course, as a tribune himself, 'guilty' of a degree of self-interest but, in a populist politician, it was probably also an attempt to emphasise the central importance of the people's will. It is hardly surprising that the word *popularis* ('mob-panderer') came to be used of such politicians by their opponents – not that they, in many cases, were much different. Again, however, it is important not to regard *populares* as, in any sense, a 'political party'.

In order to try to secure some improvement of the lot of Italians, Gaius Gracchus introduced a franchise bill that was relatively modest, presumably in the hope that the modesty of the measure would recommend it to those who saw that something had to be done, but who were fearful and suspicious of anything too radical. It appears that Gracchus' bill proposed that Latins should be 'upgraded' to full citizenship and that something less would be done for other Italians. However, like many compromises this seems to have pleased nobody, and it fell.

The equestrian order figured in two reforms of Gracchus: he replaced the senatorial members of the juries of the *quaestio de repetundis* with equestrians who, of course, did not have the close relationship with senators that had led to miscarriages of justice in the past. Further, he proposed that, in the arrangements for the new province of Asia (formerly the kingdom of Pergamum), the right to collect taxes should be auctioned in Rome amongst wealthy non-senators (that is, members of the equestrian order). Not surprisingly, this had the effect of introducing tension between the two orders, although it is likely that Gracchus was driven by two motives – the need to keep senatorial corruption under control and, perhaps, the creation within the plebeian class of an identifiable group of rich and articulate men who could be looked to as a sounder basis of support in the *concilium plebis*; in its turn, this may have been intended as a means of taking some steam out of the 'charge' of populism.

Nonetheless, Gaius Gracchus' support began to fail; as with his brother, supporters began to melt away. Of men of weight possibly only Fulvius Flaccus remained loyal. It appears that Gracchus' plans for the province of Africa may have proved to be the 'last straw': in a desire to achieve new settlement in the prosperous lands of the province, he proposed the foundation of a *colonia* – the first overseas – on the cursed site of Carthage, which had been abandoned after its destruction in 146. In mounting unpopularity, Gracchus failed to secure re-election to a third term as tribune for 121; out of office, he saw attacks mounted on elements of his legislation. This led to violence in the streets, and the consul, Lucius Opimius, obtained what has been styled the 'ultimate decree' (*senatus consultum ultimum*), which was used – against the spirit of Gracchus' own law on *provocatio* – as a means of destroying him. In the violence that ensued, Flaccus was killed and Gracchus took his own life. Although a considerable amount of his legislation remained in place, the senatorial aristocracy had in effect emerged victorious over those of its own class who had tried to use popular power against it.

The senate's relief at the removal of its 'enemy' did not last long; once again, it found itself undermined by a failing of its own – this time on the battlefield. On the borders of Africa, the capable Jugurtha had emerged as king with, it was alleged, the corrupt help of certain senators. The anti-senatorial mood was exacerbated by the fact that some Italian equestrian businessmen had been killed by Jugurtha. In an effort to restore its credibility, the senate sent as commander in Africa, Quintus Caecilius Metellus, the consul of 109 who was to achieve the title 'Numidicus'. Accompanying Metellus was an Italian equestrian from Arpinum, Gaius Marius, who had started out on a senatorial career as a 'new man' (*novus homo*), with the help of Metellus and members of his family and friends. Once in Africa, Marius saw his chance: he returned to Rome to seek a consulship for 107, arguing that Metellus was incompetent and that he would finish this trouble-some war himself. Marius not only won his consulship but, irregularly, obtained the African command by a vote of the plebeians (*plebiscitum*). He assembled a legionary army which included land-less Roman citizens (*capitecensi*): the setting aside of the property qualification, whilst justifiable in military terms and not without precedent in emergencies, was to have far-reaching implications for the republic.

Marius reformed the organisation and tactics of the army, and managed to defeat Jugurtha, although only after the Numidian had been betrayed to Marius' quaestor, Lucius Cornelius Sulla. Marius was elected, again irregularly, to a second consulship for 104 – just in time to face a major military threat in Italy itself. The north Germanic tribes, the Cimbri and the Teutones, had been creating disturbance and defeating Roman armies in western

Europe since 113; for many, Marius represented the only hope of preventing the overrunning of the Italian homeland. Three more consulships followed in successive years as Marius defeated first the Teutones (at Aquae Sextiae in 102) and the Cimbri in the following year at Vercellae in northern Italy. Italy had been saved, and Marius reached the pinnacle of his fame with a sixth consulship in 100.

However, associated with Marius were two populist politicians, Lucius Appuleius Saturninus and Gaius Servilius Glaucia; already, in 103, Saturninus had by *plebiscitum* settled veterans of Marius' African army on land in Africa, having first 'introduced' some of them into the Forum in Rome in a show of his 'muscle'. For the first time, the real danger for the republic inherent in Marius' reform of military recruiting practice was clearly visible: the landless soldiers had no land to which to return upon demobilisation, and thus depended upon a land settlement. No institutional provision was made for this eventuality; thus, on every occasion, the ex-soldiers needed a politician – their own general or someone else – to carry a land bill on their behalf to provide land upon which they could be settled. There is no suggestion, however, that Marius himself had intended by his reform to create a problem whereby the republic was effectively placed at the mercy of the relationship between its armies and generals/politicians – a 'vicious nexus', as it has been described. However, Marius was preoccupied with his wars, leaving Saturninus and Glaucia free to make the political running; in the course of this the appointment of the jury panels of the *quaestio de repetundis* became, as it was to remain during the first half of the first century, a 'political football'. Given equestrian juries by Gaius Gracchus, control of the court was restored to senators in 106, and then returned to equestrians by Glaucia in 101.

In 100, with Saturninus as tribune and Glaucia praetor, dealings between the populists and their opponents again became fraught: bills were framed to grant land in northern Italy and in the provinces to Marius' veterans, and to restore Gaius Gracchus' grain provisions. In rioting that ensued, the senate again passed a *senatus consultum ultimum*. This placed Marius, as consul, in the impossible position of having to enforce the senate's decree against his own allies; in fact, despite surrendering, Saturninus and Glaucia were stoned to death; their legislation was effectively dropped and, in the aftermath of these events, a law was passed (in 98) in an effort to prevent politicians putting packages of legislation together into a single law.

Marius had been shown to be ineffective as a politician, perhaps because, as a 'new man', he lacked weighty allies: further, in 100, he demonstrated disloyalty (*perfidia*) to those who were his allies and supporters. Scarcely a popular hero now, and unwanted by the aristocracy, Marius' position was not tenable, and he went into eclipse – to emerge a decade later to wreak a terrible revenge on those who had, in his view, despised and destroyed him.

It is probable that Italians had entertained hopes that a consul with an Italian background would have proved to be concerned about their complaints. This was not so and, in the wake of Marius' eclipse, the Italian position remained without a solution. In fact, in the 90s a measure passed against those who had assumed citizenship illegally was followed by a move by Marcus Livius Drusus, a tribune of 91, as a part of a now-illegal package of provisions, to grant Roman citizenship to all Italians. Drusus' motives are unclear, though he may have hoped that, by tying his franchise measure to others, he would provide 'something for everyone' and so disarm opposition. If so, it was not to be: the legislation was declared illegal and, later in the year, Drusus was murdered in his own home. This was an obvious signal to Italians that political pressure was achieving nothing; before 91 was out, Italians, though without the Latins and the Etruscan states, had risen in revolt in what is known as the 'Social War'. The Italians effectively set up a 'rival state', based upon Corfinium, now renamed Italica. Although they put up a hard fight and caused Rome some military embarrassment, as well as financial difficulty, the eventual outcome, with Rome's military response led by Lucius Cornelius Sulla, was hardly in doubt; in 90, Rome attempted to defuse the situation by granting the franchise to those who had not revolted; in the following year, the concession was extended to all Italians living south of the river Po; those living north of the river (the 'Transpadanes') were left out. Even so, Rome moved to limit the effect of the new citizens by confining them to a restricted number of the thirty-five voting tribes in the assemblies.

Before the Italian crisis was even settled, Rome found herself facing an even more serious threat in the eastern Mediterranean: the immediate author of this crisis was one of the most illustrious of Alexander's Hellenistic successors – Mithridates VI, king of Pontus, who appears to have entertained the ambition of embracing Greece and the Hellenistic kingdoms of Asia Minor in an anti-Roman crusade. Aggravated by Rome's treatment of him, Mithridates found fuel for his rebellion in the effects on the area, particularly in the new province of Asia, of the rapacious activities of Roman tax collectors and moneylenders who, as we have seen, had been given their opportunity by Gaius Gracchus. In addition, during the second century, Rome had removed from the eastern Mediterranean most naval power on which she could have called for assistance; the principal naval power in the region now lay in the hands of Mithridates himself and of his allies, the pirates who had their bases on the rocky coasts of southern Asia Minor (Lycia and Cilicia). These men were mostly victims of political intolerance and injustice in various states of the eastern Mediterranean who had taken refuge in a life of naval piracy. As we shall see later, before long the pirates were to become a threat throughout the Mediterranean coastal lands.

Through 89, Mithridates swept through Asia Minor and into Greece; in the province of Asia, in particular, large numbers of Romans were massacred. This new 'liberation of Hellas' saw Roman control virtually destroyed in the region. The timing could not have been worse: with Rome and her leading general, Cornelius Sulla, heavily involved in the Italian 'Social War' there was little that could immediately be done. It even appears that there may have been some kind of collusive connection between Mithridates and Marius; the latter perhaps hoped that out of the chaos he could engineer a 'comeback' as Rome's 'saviour' once again.

Sulla was one of the consuls for 88, and the conduct of the Mithridatic War had already been designated to him, even though he was still involved in the 'dying embers' of the 'Social War'; indeed, his army – the army that he was to lead against Mithridates – was still fighting at Nola in the south. Meanwhile, Marius had joined forces with the latest in the line of populist tribunes, Publius Sulpicius Rufus, who was already engaged in a campaign to distribute the votes of the new Italian citizens more evenly throughout the tribal assemblies. Sulpicius now proposed, amidst violence, that the Mithridatic command should be transferred from Sulla to Marius, although when the latter's officers went to Nola to take command of Sulla's army they were routed. Sulla, indeed, was effectively turning this army into a personal force by arguing that Marius – if he took over – would dismiss them and that, in any case, rewards under Marius' command would be far less substantial than under Sulla's.

With the loyalty of his army assured, Sulla now stated that, as consul, it was his primary duty to free Rome from the Marian rebels. The 'freeing' of Rome, however, was Sulla's revenge: Marius and Sulpicius Rufus were declared 'public enemies' (*hostes*), and together with their supporters were driven out in a bloodbath. Again, the potential danger of aspects of Marius' military reforms of two decades previously had been made alarmingly obvious. Before leaving to tackle Mithridates, Sulla initiated some political reform, the objective of which was to secure the senate's position against any resurgence in his absence of the Marian rebels. In particular, he enacted that the senate should have a veto over legislation, and that the *comitia centuriata* should stand as the sole valid voice of the people of Rome. In constitutional terms, this represented a turning back of the clock of around 250 years, and it did not long survive Sulla's departure despite the latter's rather naïve attempt to persuade Lucius Cornelius Cinna, one of the new consuls for 87, to uphold the changes.

Cinna, far from complying, replicated Sulla's tactics of the previous year; despite the attempts of his consular colleague Octavius to organise a defence of Rome against him, in collaboration with a number of senators sympathetic to Sulla, Cinna re-entered Rome. With him was the now-elderly Gaius Marius, at the head of an army raised for the purpose and including some of his veterans who had been brought over from North Africa. Cinna had promised that his behaviour in Rome would be moderate, and there is no reason to doubt that this was genuinely his intention; however, the promise had taken no account of the seething bitterness which fuelled Marius' obsession with revenge. In an orgy of bloodshed, senators and equestrians were massacred, Sulla was declared a *hostis* (thus legally undermining his position in the east), and his constitutional reforms of 88 were reversed. Finally, the consuls for

86 were named as Cinna and, for the seventh time, Gaius Marius. However, the events of the previous months must have proved too much for the old general, who lived on to see just thirteen days of his final consulship.

Attempts were orchestrated in Rome to dispossess Sulla of his command; not only did these end in failure but Mithridates' high-handed behaviour in the areas that he had 'liberated', and the organisation by Lucius Licinius Lucullus of a fleet for Sulla, enabled the latter to bring the king of Pontus to terms. These left Mithridates in command of his original territories, but little else; those in the region who had resisted Mithridates were rewarded, whilst others found themselves facing huge indemnities and indignities. Sulla was now ready to make his return to Italy at the head of an army that was both successful and rewarded; its loyalty to Sulla was thus assured.

From this position of strength, Sulla offered terms to his opponents in Rome; these were rejected, leaving Sulla no realistic option but to march against them. He was joined – perhaps an ominous glimpse into the future – by the young Pompey with a privately raised army. Although Cinna was killed by his own troops, other Marians, principally Marius' son, resisted, occasioning yet more bloodshed. Finally, on 1 November 82, Sulla inflicted a major defeat on his enemies at Rome's Colline Gate; their leaders were pursued and killed. Only one survived – Quintus Sertorius who took refuge in Spain and 'lived to fight another day'.

Sulla now, in 81, had himself made dictator, though how long he held the office is unclear; however, a striking coin was issued in 80 showing an equestrian statue of Sulla, still bearing the title, though it is not easy to say whether this indicates that Sulla remained dictator or simply that the statue carried the title. There followed a thorough overhaul of the constitutional machinery, the principal objective of which was to protect the senate's supremacy and to defend it from threats. The nature of these threats, as seen in Sulla's reforms, reflects very closely the efforts made over the past fifty years by men such as the Gracchus brothers, Marius, Saturninus and Glaucia and Sulpicius Rufus – in other words, those who tried to undermine the senate for a variety of reasons, and using 'populist' tactics.

Over the years, argument has fluctuated between those who

have concentrated on the essence of Sulla's reforms and those who have looked more to his methods of approach. Certainly, the word which has constantly pursued Sulla's memory has been 'proscription', a process by which the names of individuals were publicly posted, indicating that they could be put to death without any recourse to legal procedure; such a 'reign of terror' was inevitably based upon attacking those who had opposed Sulla and/or who were wealthy. Sulla needed both freedom from opposition and resources of land and money by which he could do 'justice' to supporters, especially his veterans. A problem, as we learn from Cicero's defence of Roscius of Ameria (*Pro Roscio Amerino*), was that Sulla failed to exercise any effective control over his henchmen in the matter of how names were appended to the lists of the proscribed; there seems little doubt that some names were added for no better reason than that one or other of Sulla's supporters had 'taken a fancy' to a particular piece of property. Obviously, this exceptionally crude political weapon damaged not just the individuals concerned but also their heirs.

If Sulla behaved (or allowed his henchmen to behave) as little better than political assassins, we should not allow this to distort our understanding of what he may have been trying to achieve. The senate was enlarged, principally with members of the equestrian order; whether this was intended to make the senate a more representative body or to cut the equestrian order down to size by removing its leading figures is less clear. For the future, the ranks of the senate were to be kept up to strength by the addition of those men who had just completed their quaestorships, the annual number of which was now raised to twenty. This, of course, meant that the organising of the senate's membership would not now be the prerogative of two, possibly prejudiced, men (the censors), but would be subject, more visibly than before, to popular vote. The senate also regained control of the jury panels of the courts (*quaestiones*), and popular involvement in the judicial process through the assemblies was to be further weakened by the establishment of more *quaestiones* to deal with specific, named, offences (such as murder, poisoning, forgery, treason, bribery, peculation and assault). This reform was never repealed and clearly 'struck a chord' for its reasonable nature.

The senate was also to be protected in more specific ways: first, the *cursus honorum* (career structure for senators) was to be more firmly regulated by the insistence upon minimum ages of tenure for the various magistracies, intervals between different magistracies and iteration of the same magistracy. This new *lex annalis* was to protect the senate from such men as Marius, Saturninus and Glaucia. The tribunate of the plebeians, though not of course a magistracy, was subjected to restrictions: for example, it seems that the use of the veto was constrained and, even more damagingly, those who held the office were to be barred from holding any further office in the future. The senate was in this way protected from the whims of populist politicians; indeed, it may be that Sulla also sought to revive the restrictions on the tribally based assemblies (*comitia populi tributa; concilium plebis*), and to insist on the necessity of senatorial approval of all measures to be brought before the people.

Finally, in what appears to have been an attempt to remove the conditions which had allowed men like himself to march on Rome from a provincial base, he introduced tight rules for promagistrates – that they should not leave their provinces during their year of office, that they should leave their provinces/commands within thirty days following the due expiry date, that they should leave unaccompanied by their armies, and that they should not engage in hostilities in their provinces without the senate's permission. His regulation of the *cursus honorum* had already ensured that there would be sufficient ex-consuls and ex-praetors available to fill the provincial vacancies without recourse to extraordinary appointments. This in its turn was intended to obviate the need for consuls and praetors during their years of office to take command of armies. The senate, probably since the time of Gaius Gracchus, had been empowered to decide in advance of the relevant elections which of the provinces should be 'reserved' for former consuls.

This was intended to ensure the supremacy and security of the senate in Rome; whilst no attempt was made to revoke the recent citizenship grants made to Italians, the military security of Italy was heightened by a revival of the programme of planting *coloniae*, in which the settlers were, of course, Sulla's veterans. Pompeii became one such *colonia* at this time.

In 79, Sulla retired from Rome; the reasons that may have lain behind this move were not clear, and we are informed by the satirist, Juvenal, that a century-and-a-half later they were still a 'debating-point'. Certainly, for the moment at least, Sulla's supporters were in the ascendant both in power and wealth. Sulla had created, it seemed, a framework which could guarantee the senate's political supremacy; he had provided answers to the problems thrown up in the physical expansion of Rome. But the 'solutions' had been constructed without any allowance for human nature. During the fifty years that separated the Gracchi from Sulla, men's ambitions had been sharpened and they had learned a variety of ways in which these could be satisfied. The passage of Sulla's laws could not destroy the ambitions nor could they banish the accumulated experience of how they could be achieved. Sulla may have already been ill when he retired – he died within a year of his retirement. He could also have appreciated that those 'who sow the wind shall reap the whirlwind'. He may, in other words, have realised that, whilst he had produced a framework that appeared plausible, he had also created a great deal of dissatisfaction – even revulsion – at what he had done and the way in which he had done it.

In retrospect, Julius Caesar was to observe that, by resigning his dictatorship, Sulla simply demonstrated his political *naïveté*. By Caesar's time it was becoming clearer that the republic could survive only by the introduction of a degree of centralisation into its government; the outstanding question came to concern the form that this should take. Had Sulla recognised this, or did he simply regard his input as perhaps the last chance to avoid it? Whether the supposed indications of a personality cult around Sulla offer any kind of an answer to this particular question is hard to say. It is clear, however, that the next decades – the last of the 'old republic' – were to make it clear that the stability which had been noted by Polybius in the government of magistrates, senate and people could not be maintained without change; the period between the Gracchi and Sulla shows clearly enough why this was.

# 4

# THE RISE AND DOMINATION OF POMPEY

The name of Gnaeus Pompeius Magnus (Pompey) stands large over all that happened in the three decades that followed Sulla's retirement from Rome; Pompey's power rose to a pinnacle in the mid-to-late 60s, only to be lost again to Julius Caesar in the early 40s. It has commonly been said of Pompey that, whilst he may have been a great general, he was no match for others in the political arena. In the Roman republic such a distinction is to an extent unreal; our sources, however, reveal a figure who achieved what he wanted in politics more often than not.

Pompey came from Picenum, to the north-east of Rome on Italy's Adriatic coast; it has been shown that men from Picenum or with Picene connections continued to play an important role for Pompey throughout his career. He was born in 106, in the same year as his friend and great admirer Marcus Tullius Cicero. The son of the uncongenial Pompeius Strabo, who had commanded armies in the 'Social War', Pompey first came to prominence when he lent his support and that of his privately raised army to Sulla during the latter's march on Rome in 83–82. Pompey was then twenty-three years of age, too young yet to hold magisterial office and therefore unqualified to hold a military command.

It has been noted that although severe difficulties stood in the way of Sulla's constitution, these were exacerbated by the arrogance and corruption of many of the *Sullani*. Indeed, in the first year (78) following Sulla's retirement, Marcus Aemilius Lepidus, who had been an implacable foe of the Marian cause, became consul with a programme which included the restoration of the tribunate; this is said to have had the support of Pompey. Whatever Lepidus' motives, he fell out with his fellow-consul (Quintus Lutatius Catulus) and, with his deputy (*legatus*), Marcus Junius Brutus, began raising troops in Italy. Early in 77, Lepidus marched his army on Rome; the senate passed the *senatus consultum ultimum* and gave Pompey the status – either a propraetorian *imperium* or a *legatio* – to enable him to deploy his private army against Lepidus and Brutus, despite having so recently supported them. Indeed, he was responsible for Brutus' execution, a fact that Brutus' family did not allow him to forget.

It was soon apparent that this encouragement of Pompey represented a serious error of judgement: when, following his defeat of Brutus, he was instructed by Catulus to disband his army, Pompey's response was that he should be sent to Spain with an extraordinary proconsular *imperium* to aid Metellus Pius in the eradication of the remnants of Marius' supporters, who were under the command of the talented Quintus Sertorius. The senate conceded: thus Pompey, despite still not having senatorial status, now enjoyed the standing of an ex-consul on a level with Metellus Pius. This, of course, was precisely the kind of irregularity that Sulla had sought to prevent, and the fact that Pompey did restore peace in Spain could not alter the political damage which such an appointment had inflicted. Nevertheless, it could not be denied that Sertorius was a real danger: he inspired loyalty, had trained an efficient army and had created a kind of Roman state in Iberia.

With one exception, the problems of the 70s remained in the foreign and military fields (see Figure 3); that exception, however, was important. We have seen that Sulla had acted in a particularly punitive way against the office of tribune of the plebeians; this presumably explains why a reaction appeared so soon. As we have seen, the debate opened in the consulship of Lepidus (78) and by the mid-70s there was a not-inconsiderable campaign underway, although for obvious reasons its leading lights were generally younger members of the nobility. It is possible that Julius Caesar, whose patrician status rendered him personally ineligible for the office, may have been influenced to support it by his mother,

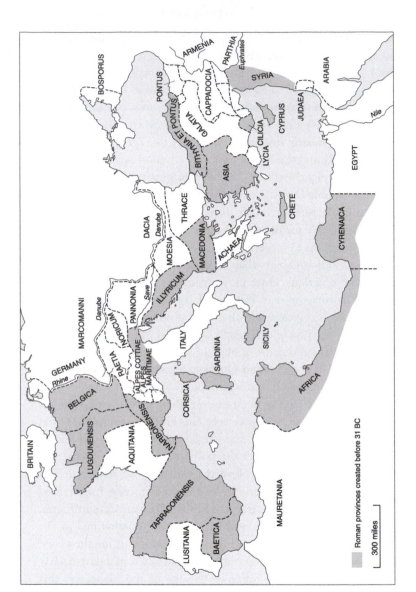

*Figure 3* The Roman empire in the late first century BC

Roman provinces created before 31 BC

300 miles

Aurelia. In any case, Caesar tended at this early stage of his career to identify himself as the enemy of the authoritarianism and corruption which had characterised the Sullan age. The 70s were proving to be a lawless decade, with pirate raids on the coast and Sulla's former supporters, already rich from the pickings of proscription, fighting each other with gangs of slaves for ownership of land in Italy. Although this lawlessness may have prompted the small concessions to the plebeians which were forthcoming in the matter of the future of the tribunate, a full restoration of the office and its privileges had to await the joint consulship of Pompey and Crassus in 70.

Caesar was also involved in unsuccessful attempts to prosecute notoriously corrupt provincial governors. These cases highlighted the venality of the courts, the juries of which, since Sulla's time, had been dominated by senators; one such case, however, was successful – that brought in 70 against Gaius Verres by the people of Sicily, who secured the services of one of Rome's greatest advocates, Marcus Cicero, to prosecute the case. This was Cicero's first major oration as a prosecutor, and it set him on a course which was to take him to a position of considerable influence in the republic's later years. This case also contributed to the growing awareness of the vicious corruption that surrounded many of Sulla's supporters and did little to enhance the reputation of the senatorial nobility.

In three further military episodes, 'rules' laid down by Sulla were breached: in 74, a special command was given to Marcus Antonius (the father of Julius Caesar's associate) to bring the pirates of the Mediterranean under control. Piracy had been a growing problem since the eclipse of the great navies belonging to the states of mainland Greece; it had become a great deal worse since Rome's intervention in the eastern Mediterranean in the second century BC which had led to the elimination of navies such as that of Rhodes, especially as no adequate alternative was put in place. More recently, the pirates had gained added stature from their alliance with Mithridates. By the 70s, as we have seen, they were able to operate almost without limit in the Mediterranean, even attacking coastal Italy. Antonius proved ineffectual, and the problem remained as serious as ever. The fear and anger that it precipitated were to lead to the extensive command granted to Pompey in 67.

In the same year (74) it became clear that fresh action would be required to keep Mithridates under control. In the previous year, Rome's 'friend and ally', Nicomedes of Bithynia, had willed his kingdom to Rome; the senate's acceptance of the bequest provided the signal for Mithridates himself to aim a pre-emptive strike at Bithynia. In response, the incumbent consuls of 74, Marcus Aurelius Cotta and Lucius Licinius Lucullus, were sent to the area – Cotta in charge of Bithynia and Lucullus of the provinces of Asia and Cilicia, together with the conduct of the actual war against Mithridates.

The last of these military problems – the revolt in Italy itself of the Thracian gladiator, Spartacus, in 73 – proved to be the catalyst to a major attack on Sulla's constitutional arrangements. Spartacus' revolt came as the culmination of years of unrest between gangs of slaves; he caused considerable disruption in Italy and defeated the consuls of 72 who had been sent against him. The republic's armies were thus left under the command of the man whose name was to be associated with Pompey's over the next two decades, Marcus Licinius Crassus, one of the praetors of 73. He fared better, defeating and killing Spartacus, though not before the senate and people, in something of a panic, had voted that Crassus should share his command with Pompey, freshly returned from Spain. To Crassus' annoyance, Pompey claimed half of the glory, even though his contribution in reality had been little more than to mop up a few remnants after Spartacus' defeat.

Some senators may have hoped that their own political salvation would be secured by Pompey and Crassus turning their armies against each other: no love had ever been lost between these two former supporters of Sulla, and Crassus, along with others, would have been viewing Pompey's illegal and opportunistic rise during the 70s with envy and disquiet. Such anxieties were more than confirmed by Pompey's arrogance in the war against Spartacus. However, the expected denouement was not to be; instead, these two rivals decided to form a temporary political partnership (*amicitia*), pooling their wealth, their armies and their clientage in a bid for the consulship of 70 with a programme which involved undoing much of what was left of Sulla's constitutional arrangements. The coalition of interests and resources was powerfully coercive; Crassus and Pompey found little difficulty in securing acquiescence to their requirements. In addition, Pompey was given a triumph for his successes in Spain, whilst Crassus gained an ovation for his against Spartacus.

Crassus, having held a praetorship in 73, was, under the terms of Sulla's *lex annalis*, qualified to hold the consulship; Pompey, on the other hand, needed an exemption as he was too young and had held none of the qualifying offices; in fact, he was still not even a member of the senate. Their programme of legislation went a long way to restoring the pre-Sullan status quo: the powers of the tribunate were restored in full to boost confidence that corruption in and out of politics might now be tackled seriously. The lawlessness of the 70s, and in particular the high-profile case against Gaius Verres, emphasised just how much needed to be done. Although Verres had, in fact, been convicted by a senatorial jury, this was more a tribute to the skill and persistence of Cicero than to the integrity of the jurors. Pompey and Crassus altered the composition of the jury panels of the *quaestiones*: senators were not to be excluded from them, but would make up just one-third of the panels, sharing the responsibility with equestrians and other wealthy men. Further, although Sulla had not abolished the office of censor, none had been elected since before his time; in 70, censors were elected to office and accelerated the enrolment of Italians into the citizenship. It is also a measure of the recognised corruption of the senatorial aristocracy at this stage that more than sixty senators were expelled from membership by the new censors. As further evidence of the deep-seated nature of this corruption, we may cite the extensive programme of legislation aimed at it in 67 by the tribunes Gaius Cornelius and Aulus Gabinius, the latter of whom was certainly an associate of Pompey.

Aside from internal corruption, the major issues which continued to trouble the republic into the 60s were relations with Mithridates and piracy; as before, the two were not unconnected, as pirates were able to effect communication for Mithridates with all parts of the Mediterranean. Since 74, the war against Mithridates had been in the hands of the capable Sullan, Lucius Licinius Lucullus; by 70, he had Mithridates 'on the ropes' and close to defeat; but he began to find the network of Mithridates' associates and the extent of territory over which he was consequently expected to operate to be too great, resulting in his simply asking too much of his troops; Lucullus' effectiveness as commander was unable to survive this. Second, Lucullus had tried to alleviate the financial hardship that had overtaken the provincials of Asia, which had come about partly as a result of Mithridates' activities in the area and partly because of the harshness of Sulla's settlement in the mid-80s.

However, alleviating the lot of provincials could not be achieved without reducing the 'profit margins' of Roman businessmen in the area; although Lucullus was remembered as something of a hero in Asia – a festival was named after him – there was a groundswell of opinion in Rome that the time had come to be rid of him, which has all the appearance of an orchestrated campaign; indeed, Lucullus' own brother-in-law, Publius Claudius Pulcher (who preferred to be called 'Clodius', the popular form of his name), who was among his entourage, set out to create disaffection in Lucullus' already demoralised army. How far (if at all) Pompey and Crassus were involved in this is unclear, but the campaign culminated in laws passed by the tribunes Aulus Gabinius (67) and Gaius Manilius (66); the former created a command for Pompey, as well as removing from Lucullus the province of Bithynia/Pontus, whilst the latter transferred to Pompey the remainder of the command held by Lucullus. The 'bad blood' that is subsequently evident in the relationship of Pompey and Lucullus certainly suggests that the latter, at least, believed that Pompey had been behind the campaign to remove him.

By the 70s and 60s, as we have seen, the pirates were far more than simply a nuisance in the eastern Mediterranean. From their bases on the rocky and inaccessible coasts of Cilicia and Crete, they not only aided major enemies such as Mithridates but disrupted normal shipping – and thus supplies of food and other commodities – throughout the Mediterranean. Rome's earlier attempts to deal with the problem in 102 and again in 74 had achieved little; nor had the most recent effort, from 68 to 67, by Quintus Metellus (Creticus), who formally added Crete as a province to the empire. It was obviously in everyone's interests – politicians, businessmen, ordinary consumers – that this problem be eradicated without further delay. Such a task, if successfully completed, would bring with it enormous opportunities for enhancement of reputation, wealth and patronage.

Gabinius' main bill (the *lex Gabinia* of 67) was to create a special command with authority throughout the Mediterranean and with vast resources, and to award it to a former consul. It is (and, of course, was) clear that Pompey was meant; those amongst the tribunes who tried to oppose or modify the bill were treated by Gabinius as Tiberius Gracchus had treated Octavius in 133. Pompey got his command: clearly he relished a military and organisational challenge on this scale, and he will also have welcomed the fact that considerable patronage was now his to dispense: Gabinius' bill allowed for the appointment of twenty-four 'deputies' (*legati*), men who would as a result be regarded as under obligation to Pompey. Within three months, Pompey had solved the pirate problem and, as in Spain during the 70s, he demonstrated his statesmanship by putting in place a sensitive and thoughtful programme of post-war resettlement of the pirates which was designed to ensure prolonged stability.

Cicero's rhetoric in the aftermath of this achievement was ecstatic: the whole world could heave a great sigh of relief and once again have confidence in family, home and property. For Cicero, who, like Marius, was an Italian from Arpinum, and whose forensic success had carried him (aged only 40) to a praetorship for 66, it was obvious that Pompey was now the republic's only guarantor of prosperity and stability; thus, in his surviving speech in support of Manilius' tribunician bill (*Pro Lege Manilia*), he threw himself behind the proposition that Lucullus' command against Mithridates should be transferred to Pompey. Once again, Pompey delivered successfully, although Lucullus, who was predictably unimpressed, referred to Pompey as 'the carrion-bird who feasted on the leftovers of others'. It is certainly true that Lucullus had blunted Mithridates at the height of his power, whilst the Mithridates whom Pompey faced and who committed suicide in 63, after nearly sixty years on his throne, was but a shadow of his former self. Again, Pompey followed military success with a wise post-war settlement which depended on the creation of a network of provinces around the coasts of Asia Minor, with client kingdoms in the interior.

Pompey was now at the summit of his military reputation, a position which brought with it great wealth and ability to dispense patronage; unsurprisingly, it was also viewed by some with envy and disquiet. Some members of the aristocracy will have continued to smart over the treatment of Lucullus, whilst others sought, where possible, to erode Pompey's influence and standing (*auctoritas*), recalling the self-seeking irregularity of his earlier career in the 70s. Crassus, for example, tended to work from behind the scenes, manipulating people to operate in his interests: it would not be surprising if, at this stage, he was concerned to engineer for himself a position in which Pompey would have to take him seriously as a political force; nor was he averse to undermining Pompey's support where he could.

As censor in 65, Crassus first tried to give full citizenship to the Italians living beyond the river Po (Transpadane Gaul), who had been left out of the settlement which followed the 'Social War'; this was an area in which Pompey had some influence because of his father's patronal interests, and which might prove valuable for its manpower. Crassus failed in this venture, as he may have anticipated, but was remembered for his attempt. Second, Crassus organised a special command for Gnaeus Calpurnius Piso in Spain, an area with good memories of Pompey from the 70s. Whilst it remains unclear precisely what was at stake, the historian Sallust leaves the broad issue in little doubt when he informs us that Piso was murdered by friends of Pompey. Third, Crassus became involved in the affairs of Egypt, though whether as a proponent or as a supporter of someone else is unclear. The objective appears to have been an attempt to add Egypt to the empire as a province; the wealth of the kingdom would have made it, as it was to prove later for the emperor Augustus, an attractive place in which to hold influence; Egypt also played a key role in Rome's grain supply and in other commercial activities. Again, the move failed, not least because of the involvement of Cicero who, in a partly preserved speech (*De Rege Alexandrino*), argued that the whole matter represented an attempt to weaken Pompey. If any or all of these were Crassus' initiatives, they appear to have yielded little.

If these events are hard to interpret, a far larger problem surrounds a series of incidents in Rome between 66 and 63, most of which in some way appear to have involved a patrician senator, Lucius Sergius Catilina (usually known as 'Catiline'), who had at one time been a supporter of Sulla. There is also some epigraphic evidence to suggest that there had been a connection between

Catiline and Pompey's father, although it is unclear whether this was of any relevance to Catiline's conduct in the 60s.

Catiline is, of course, best known for the conspiracy which he headed in 63, the year in which Cicero was consul; it seems likely that he was a less-than-savoury character and that these two facts have worked to make him a candidate for inclusion in any suspicious episode. The first of these is the so-called 'first conspiracy of Catiline' which allegedly took place at the turn of the years 66 and 65. The fact that it is difficult to establish the truth now is largely due to the paucity of facts at the time and [to Cicero's readiness to embellish the affair.] In two places – in his own election speech (*Oratio in Toga Candida*) in 64 and in his Orations against Catiline in the following year – Cicero alleged that on 1 January 65, Catiline was in the Forum with a dagger ready to assassinate the incoming consuls Lucius Aurelius Cotta and Lucius Manlius Torquatus.

The incident appears to have sprung from the disqualification for electoral corruption of the two candidates who were originally successful – Publius Autronius Paetus and Publius Cornelius Sulla (the dictator's nephew). Catiline, it is suggested, had wished to be a candidate, but had been disqualified from standing because of an unresolved charge of malpractice which derived from his term as propraetor in Africa in 67. Cotta and Torquatus emerged as the successful candidates in a re-run election, but action was allegedly planned to assassinate them and, according to which version is followed, to replace them with any two of Autronius, Sulla and Catiline.

We should bear in mind that this event occurred at a time when attacks had been launched on corruption in government; in these circumstances, a plot or, at least, a demonstration by Autronius and Sulla, stemming from the loss of their consulships, is intelligible, but Catiline's involvement is much less so; furthermore, we learn from subsequent references by Cicero that later in 65 the orator was himself planning to offer to defend Catiline on his outstanding misgovernment charge – an offer that was refused – and that, in fact, Catiline was defended by Torquatus, the man whom allegedly he had been planning to assassinate. It would seem that either the allegation against Catiline was a fabrication or, perhaps, that Catiline was present – but to defend Torquatus, not to harm him. It appears that Torquatus at this

time had a connection with Pompey; one wonders whether perhaps Catiline did also. Allegations were also made, but not sub-
stantiated, that Crassus and Caesar were involved in the events at
the beginning of 65.

Cicero's offer to defend Catiline was connected with the fact
that, in 64, they would both be seeking a consulship for 63;
Cicero presumably realised that Catiline would be a better ally
than an opponent. However, Catiline's refusal to accept Cicero's
offer meant that, as a 'new man', Cicero had a real fight on his
hands; his *Oratio in Toga Candida*, which survives only in fragmentary form, represents an attempt at a comprehensive demoli-
tion of Catiline's credibility as a candidate. It is probable that
it was his apprehension about the opposition that led Cicero to
support at this time a campaign to win for Lucullus a well-
deserved triumph for his achievements in the east; it is unlikely
that Pompey will have had much sympathy for this enterprise.

Cicero was elected, along with Gaius Antonius, the uncle of
Julius Caesar's later associate. Catiline will have been angry to
have been worsted by the 'man from Arpinum', but there is no
evidence to suggest that he was, as yet, so desperate as to turn to
conspiracy; for the moment, at least, he lived to fight another day
– that is, in the elections to be held in 63. Cicero immediately
found himself pitched into further controversy: one of the new
tribunes, who had taken office in December of 64, Publius Servilius
Rullus, proposed a land bill; it is difficult to determine now what
the purpose of this was, or whether any sinister machinations lay
behind it, although Cicero talked darkly of Rullus 'and those
whom you fear more than you do Rullus', hinting that its purpose
was to cause embarrassment to Pompey. It is known that debt and
financial distress were at a peak in the late 60s, and it is possible
that Rullus was principally concerned with land redistribution –
something with which Cicero, with his innate respect for the
integrity of property ownership, never had much sympathy. It is
also possible that, since Rullus had evidently had some connection
with Pompey in the mid-60s, the bill was also intended to 'pre-
pare the ground' for the settlement that would be required when
Pompey returned from the east with his army. The failure of
Rullus' bill will, in that case, have created for Pompey difficulties
which he could well have done without.

The major event of Cicero's consulship in 63, however, was the conspiracy headed by Catiline, which occupied the second half of the year. Initially, it was evidently Catiline's intention to stand again for election with a view to becoming one of the consuls for 62. Cicero continued against him the campaign of 'character assassination' which had been a feature of the consul's election pitch during the previous year, stressing the havoc and ruin that threatened the republic in the event of Catiline's election. In view of the fact that debt cancellation was a plank of Catiline's programme, Cicero, as always hostile to such policies, predictably stressed the disturbance of financial order that would be precipitated by Catiline's election. By rhetoric and by ruse, Cicero had his way, and Catiline suffered another defeat. The humiliation and frustration of this at last appear to have prompted this former supporter of Sulla to attempt to override constitutional proprieties and take power by force.

Catiline's insurrection was evidently planned for the last days of October; it is tempting to see Cicero as heading a great 'national crusade' to destroy this threat to life and liberty, but the reality seems to have been that there was a general reluctance to believe the consul, especially with Catiline himself sitting in the senate, baiting Cicero, well informed though he was, to act against him. It was only on 21 October that, armed with evidence that Catiline was planning his assassination, he at last persuaded the senators to pass a *senatus consultum ultimum* against Catiline; even so, Catiline did not leave Rome until the beginning of November, and then like a general to take command of his army. The reality of the situation is significant, because Cicero was to build so many of his hopes for the future on the notion that all along he enjoyed the willing and general support of 'all good men' (*optimates*).

Catiline now appears to have replanned his revolution on two fronts: first, the city's population had increased considerably in the second and first centuries, and a significant part of this increase had been caused by the influx of slaves; Catiline proposed to stir up a slave rebellion in Rome – an event which he seems to have planned to coincide with the Saturnalia festival on 17 December, at which time slaves were traditionally allowed a greater degree of licence in their behaviour than was usual. Such a threat was potentially extremely disruptive. Second, a 'military attack' was planned from outside the city, with Catiline's associate, Manlius, recruiting peasant farmers, many of whom had been settled on land after Sulla's wars but who had not managed to make a success of farming and were now eager for a way out of their difficulties.

Cicero's patience was rewarded when some members of a delegation from the Gallic tribe of the Allobroges, who had been approached on Catiline's behalf, reported to the consul what they knew; as a result, a number of Catiline's associates in Rome were arrested on the night of 2/3 December. They were interrogated in the senate on 3 December and, two days later, a meeting of the senate discussed their fate – a debate which is prominently featured in Sallust's account of the conspiracy. As consul, Cicero presided over the debate; it was no secret that he wanted them executed, and believed that the earlier passage of the *senatus consultum ultimum*, albeit against Catiline himself, made this inevitable (as well as desirable). In fact, the senate was not a court and, therefore, had no competence to try the men; its function was simply to advise upon which of the *quaestiones* was competent – in this case, that dealing with murder or that with riot.

Sallust shows that the earlier speakers in the debate (the consuls-designate and ex-consuls) favoured the imposition of the death penalty (which was, in any case, illegal because it ignored the men's *provocatio*, as well as the fact that the original senatorial decree had been directed just against Catiline); the 'praetorian group' followed, of whom, in Sallust's account, the most prominent and eloquent was Julius Caesar who advised caution on the grounds of legality. Caesar, however, proposed the non-existent and, therefore, equally illegal penalty of 'life-imprisonment'; clearly, he was anxious, in the interests of his own credibility, to steer a course between illegality and a softness which some would interpret as evidence of collusion with Catiline. Unusually, the debate continued further, and the 'tribunician group' was heard: Marcus Cato, whom Cicero later dubbed 'our hero' for his role on the day, returned to a ringing endorsement of the death penalty, and this carried the day. On the night of 5 December, the Catilinarians who had been arrested were put to death; early in 62, Catiline himself was killed 'in the field' at the head of his army.

There is no doubt that, as Caesar had warned and as had also emerged earlier in the year in the trial of Gaius Rabirius, it was a dubious proposition that the passage of a *senatus consultum ultimum* and a senatorial vote could legally clear the way for the consul to execute Roman citizens: it was a matter which would return to haunt Cicero. For the moment, however, the consul was basking in glory: a grateful populace conferred upon him the title of 'Father of his Country' (*Pater Patriae*), despite the fact that some in the senate, such as Quintus Metellus Nepos (tribune in 62) and Julius Caesar (praetor in 62), were making clear their misgivings over Cicero's conduct: it was even suggested that Pompey should be recalled from the east to put down the tyranny of Cicero. It remains unclear whether such attacks in any sense represented the views of the absent Pompey.

In verse and prose, in Latin and Greek, Cicero wrote fulsome accounts of his achievements in 63 – to the extent that some evidently found these a joke, whilst others – perhaps including Pompey – were aggravated by the claims made. The later satirist, Juvenal, quotes a line from the Latin verse edition, citing it as one of the worst Latin hexameter lines ever written: 'O happy the Rome that was born in the year of my consulship' (*O fortunatam natam me consule Romam*). Cicero's elation was itself born of the fact that he had saved Rome from a dangerous conspiracy and, even more importantly, that he had done this at the head of a grouping of all good men, whether senators, equestrians or ordinary citizens, in Rome and Italy. This was the *concordia ordinum* (Union of the Orders) and the *consensus bonorum* (harmony of good men) which Cicero hoped would marginalise men like Catiline and others with 'unpatriotic' ambitions and upon which Cicero was to base a great deal of his future political thinking. Immediately, he saw himself as working in concert with the absent Pompey; in a letter to Pompey, written in 62, Cicero expressed the hope that, just as Pompey would fill the role of Scipio Aemilianus, he himself might be considered as equivalent to Scipio's great friend, Gaius Laelius Sapiens. Cicero could justify this in his own mind by arguing that, just as Pompey defended Roman interests in the empire, so he (Cicero) had saved Rome from the potential devastation of Catiline's insurrection. Pompey was the man of military success, wealth, standing and a clientage of unprecedented size (*auctoritas*); he probably did not appreciate having Cicero's achievements equated with his own.

In the longer term, as we learn from Cicero's later treatise, 'On the Republic' (*De Republica*), his 'dream' of an ideal republic envisaged the government of magistrates, senate and people sound in its own integrity but protected from danger (internal and external) by the man of *auctoritas* who had no ambitions for himself apart from safeguarding Rome and her empire. In the event, however, Cicero was to discover that Pompey's ambitions were far more specific and self-interested than this, and that his 'union of good men' was far less solid and reliable than he had hoped and expected. Again, Cicero's 'good men' had aspirations of their own which did not include being given their role by a man from Arpinum, a man who had been dubbed on one occasion a 'resident alien' and described by Catiline as a man enjoying honours – that is, the consulship – of which he was 'unworthy' (that is, because of his background).

For Cicero, therefore, the elimination of Catiline meant that the republic could now return to functioning in a stable 'Polybian style'. However, the storm clouds were not long in appearing: two problems in particular, and the consequences of them, dominated the events of 62 – the desecration of the ceremony of the *Bona Dea* by Publius Clodius and Pompey's return from the east.

It remains far from clear why Clodius, disguised as a woman, gatecrashed the ceremonies held by the Vestal Virgins in honour of the *Bona Dea*, or whether they should be treated as relevant to his public or his private life. This is in part due to the fact that little is known of Clodius' career previous to 62, and partly because the repercussions soon became more momentous than the incident itself. The incident was declared sacrilegious by the senate (at Cato's urging) and Clodius put on trial; although Cicero did his best to destroy Clodius' alibi, the young patrician was acquitted as a result of substantial bribery organised by an unknown person; Cicero's 'encoded' identification of him in a letter has led some to conclude that it was Marcus Crassus. The ceremony was held at the house of the *pontifex maximus*, Julius Caesar, who was also *praetor urbanus* at the time, and it has also been suggested that the incident was aimed at embroiling him in scandal. The real damage that was done by this incident, however, derived from the bribery of the jury whose members were described by Cicero as a 'worse crew than one would find in a gambling-joint'. Since 70, the jury panels had consisted of senators, equestrians and other wealthy men: Cato, who had taken the moral high ground at the debate on the fate of the arrested Catilinarians in 63, decided, as we shall see, to turn his indignation on to the equestrian order. For Cicero, however, this rift between senators and equestrians was especially damaging to stability, and he later observed that it might have been better just to leave Clodius with a *threat* of prosecution hanging over him. For Cato and the majority of senators, the discomfiture of Cicero was of little significance.

In the midst of these events, Pompey returned from the east; some may have expected him to use his army and, following Sulla's example, take Rome by force. Instead, he disbanded it – out of a regard for the constitution, according to some, but more probably simply out of arrogance, a characteristic for which Pompey was noted. Immediately after his return, he was asked to give his views on the Clodius affair; according to Cicero, who was plainly unimpressed by the performance of his hero on this occasion, Pompey spoke about his enduring respect for the senate's authority, and took a long time to do it. Pompey, of course, could not really afford to pay overmuch attention to Cicero and his requirements, because he had his own needs: the granting of a triumph for his eastern achievements, the ratification of his eastern settlement and the allocation of land for his disbanded army.

The triumph was granted – and celebrated over two days in September 61; however, the other two requests were obstructed by Cato and his associates, perhaps to a degree out of loyalty to Lucullus. This was a severe embarrassment to Pompey: without the ratification, those to whom he had promised positions in the east and others who were looking to profit from the commercial opportunities in the new territories had to wait. Without a land settlement, Pompey would look to his former soldiers increasingly like a 'lame duck'. A further problem arose from Cato's rift with the equestrians over Clodius' trial: because of the delay in realising the new business opportunities in the east, some equestrians found that they had entered into agreements for such enterprises as tax collection, which were going to lead to financial losses for them. Consequently, they requested that their contracts be revised downwards; Crassus supported them, and Cicero backed him, not because he believed in the equestrians' cause but in an attempt to keep his coalition in being. Cato, however, argued that it was not the senate's responsibility to rescue equestrians who had simply been too greedy. Cicero, with some feeling, accused Cato of behaving as if he lived in 'Plato's Republic rather than in the sink of Romulus'; the orator knew that together these events represented a deadly blow to his political hopes of achieving stability.

Whilst Pompey and Crassus had thus, by 60, run into a senatorial wall of obstruction, a further problem arose in that year: Julius Caesar returned from his propraetorship in Spain and was looking for a triumph to mark his achievements. Men hoping to triumph were required to wait with their troops outside the city limit until such time as the request had been granted and arrangements were in place. For Caesar in 60, however, this posed a difficulty: he wished to be a candidate for the consulships of 59, but to carry this forward he needed to enter the city to present his candidature. His request to be permitted to do this *in absentia* was refused; Caesar's enemies hoped that, not wishing to forgo his triumph, he would remain outside the city.

It remains unclear when precisely Pompey, Crassus and Caesar decided to 'pool' their efforts and resources in the arrangement which we refer to as 'the first triumvirate', but which at least one contemporary, the polymath and satirist Varro, described as 'the three-headed monster'. Certainly, there appears to have been some co-operation over the matter of Caesar's consulship, as a friend of Pompey's, Lucius Lucceius, put up as Caesar's 'running-mate'; Caesar himself decided that his priority was the consulship and entered Rome to canvass. The opposition, organised evidently by Cato, was determined; Cato, who was usually to be found occupying the 'moral high ground', sanctioned widespread bribery in favour of his friend Marcus Calpurnius Bibulus. The political temperature at this point can be gauged by the fact that, whilst Caesar won a consulship, Lucceius did not. Caesar thus found himself with Bibulus as his colleague for 59.

The 60s had been Pompey's heyday; throughout the decade and, indeed, for much of that which preceded it, his figure had dominated Roman politics, and much that was done was prompted by a desire either to win his favour or to frustrate him; whilst he enjoyed a reputation on the back of which others could (and did) rise, he had also made many enemies by his own unorthodox path along the political ladder, a path that had left casualties in its wake. By the end of the 60s it may be that his influence had just peaked, for Pompey had shown during 61 and 60 that he was vulnerable to opposition. Nonetheless, to 'write him off' at this stage would be decidedly premature; the mass of his wealth and extent of his clientage meant that not only was he the driving force behind the *amicitia* with Crassus and Caesar but also that he remained the most powerful man in Rome well into the 50s. Further, his cynical attitude to loyalties and friendships placed him amongst the most unpredictable, and thus most dangerous, of the politicians of the late republic.

It was not for no reason that, early on, he had earned the sobriquet of *adulescentulus carnifex* ('youthful executioner'); nothing was allowed to stand in the way of the ambitions of Gnaeus Pompeius Magnus.

# 5

## THE 'THREE-HEADED MONSTER' AND THE SLIDE TO CIVIL WAR

As we have seen, the compact known to history as 'the first triumvirate' should not, in any sense, be likened to that formed later between Antonius, Octavian and Lepidus: that was an officially sanctioned instrument for government and oppression. The compact formed between Pompey, Crassus and Caesar was informal, personal and temporary, an *amicitia* similar to that which had been agreed in the late 70s between Pompey and Crassus. Nonetheless, the date of its establishment (60/59) was seen by contemporaries as of significance: it precipitated the slide to civil war and the end of the old republic. It was the point with which the Augustan (but very independently minded) historian, Gaius Asinius Pollio, chose to commence his history.

In the first place, there is doubt over the commencement of the pact – whether it preceded Caesar's candidature for the consulship or followed his success (both in 60), or whether it was as late as Caesar's entering upon his consulship (in 59). It certainly did not concern itself with the running of the government and was probably not intended to last beyond the fulfilment of its specific aims. These were related particularly to the problems that had been encountered by the three in the late 60s, and it was left to Caesar and to other officers of 59 who were well-disposed, such as the tribune, Publius Vatinius, to see to the required legislation. That the compact was ultimately limited in its objectives was inevitable given the fact that all three participants were essentially 'bidding' for the same popular support.

The first months of Caesar's consulship were taken up with moves to secure the resolution of the issues which had brought the three together in the first place. Their opponents in the senate, buoyant over their success in securing the election of Bibulus as Caesar's consular colleague, continued to be obstructive. Caesar was attempting to secure the passage of an agrarian law to provide land principally for distribution to Pompey's veterans, but probably to other citizens also. However, he found his way through the orthodox channels of senate and people blocked; never one to accept opposition lightly, he exercised his legal prerogative and took his bill directly to the *comitia*. Even so, he heeded genuine concerns and promised that the land commission, which was to be set up to administer the bill's working, would deal only with land that came naturally onto the market; nor would it touch the good agricultural land of Campania. Not surprisingly, some will have regarded land situated so close to Rome as an extremely sensitive location on which to settle Pompey's veterans. Besides this, the public land of Campania was currently leased out, and there was concern at the prospect of disturbing existing tenants. It was probably the poor supply of land on the terms stated, rather than vindictiveness on Caesar's part, that in April led the consul to go back on some of his undertakings and, in the *lex Campana*, to extend the commissioners' brief to land in Campania; behind much of this activity lay the implicit threat that Pompey's veterans might be introduced into Rome to accomplish what the art of persuasion could not.

Other necessary legislation was pursued by the tribune, Vatinius, in the *concilium plebis*: Pompey's eastern settlements were ratified, and one-third of the bid for the Asian tax contract was remitted to the equestrians. Vatinius also looked to Caesar's needs, which now consisted principally of a proconsulship which he considered suitable. For some time there had been indications that attention would need to be given to the stability of western Europe. As had happened in the late-second century, when the Cimbri and the Teutones had been destabilised and had swept through western Europe as far as northern Italy, population movements in central Europe were putting pressure on those adjacent to them.

In particular, Ariovistus, the chief of the Suebi who lived on the eastern bank of the Rhine, was forced to cross the river in search of new homelands; this, in its turn, put pressure on tribes in central Gaul, some of which had alliances with Rome. Similarly, the tribe of the Helvetii (of modern Switzerland) wished, for reasons similar to those of Ariovistus, to make a migration – peaceful in this case – to new homes in south-west Gaul; they hoped to be able to save time and effort by going through the Roman province of Gallia Transalpina.

Already in 60 there had been talk in Rome of the possibility of war in Gaul, although immediately this was averted by recognising Ariovistus as an ally of Rome. However, prior to the consular elections of 60, the senate had named the 'woodlands and paths' of Italy as a proconsular province for the consuls of 59. Although it has been suggested that this was a sinecure intended to 'clip the wings' of Caesar who, it was supposed, was looking for a major military command, it seems more reasonable to believe that this move was intended to leave the consuls of 59 uncommitted should war break out in Gaul.

Vatinius, in fact, secured the passage of a bill which gave Caesar command of Cisalpine Gaul and Illyricum with three legions for a period of five years; it would appear that, despite the fact that this was a *proconsular* command, its operation was dated from 1 March 59 rather than from the end of the consular year. Later in the year, at Pompey's behest, Gallia Transalpina was added to Caesar's command, although apparently under normal conditions of appointment, such as annual tenure. This perhaps indicates that fears of disturbances in Gaul continued to grow during the course of 59.

Cicero noted the growing unpopularity of the three, and observed with enthusiasm what he saw as signs that their arrangement, which he regarded as nothing short of *dominatio*, was breaking down; Pompey, he was sure, would soon come to realise that his best interests would be served by a closer relationship with the senate. Cicero evidently overlooked the strength of the bond that existed between Caesar and Pompey through the latter's marriage to Caesar's daughter, Julia. Further, whilst it was true that by the early summer the purposes for which the arrangement between the three men had come about had been fulfilled, they still had mutual interests which required protection. In addition, the three had acquired considerable sums of money with which to protect those interests through a very suspect deal by which they had recognised Ptolemy Auletes as the rightful king of Egypt.

In an atmosphere of growing tension, Cato's associates in the senate were enthusiastic in their support of Caesar's consular colleague, Marcus Bibulus, who, sensing that he was not able to control Caesar by normal means, had elected to 'watch the sky for omens', a religious manoeuvre which properly should have brought Caesar's legislative programme to a halt; in the years to come, Caesar's ignoring of Bibulus was certainly seen by many as leaving a significant question mark hanging over the legitimacy of what Caesar had done in 59.

Caesar, in particular, was intolerant of opposition, whilst Pompey was affected by a morbid fear of assassination and hated, according to Cicero, to witness signs of his unpopularity. In this situation, safeguarding their legislation became a priority for the three; an awareness of the need for this appears to have been sharpened by a speech which Cicero made in the spring of 59 defending his consular colleague of 63, Gaius Antonius. In this, the orator gave vent to his criticisms regarding the current situation, prompting Caesar and Pompey to participate in a move which was to have unexpected and profound consequences.

For some time, Publius Clodius had been attempting to secure a renunciation of his patrician status in order to become a plebeian; this *transitio ad plebem* was an essential prerequisite to his competing for the office of tribune of the plebeians. After a number of frustrated attempts to do this, Clodius' change of status was suddenly facilitated by Caesar (as *pontifex maximus*) and Pompey (as *augur*). There can be little doubt that they hoped that this would make Clodius co-operative and, as tribune in 58, ready to ward off any attacks launched by their senatorial enemies on the legislation of Caesar's consulship. In particular, they may well have been anxious regarding the intentions of Cato and Cicero, the latter having declined an original invitation to be a part of the *amicitia*.

However, Clodius had ambitions of his own: in the short term, he probably still felt that he had scores to settle with Pompey,

Cicero and Cato, the first two of whom had failed to support him on the occasion of his trial for sacrilege in 61 despite his earlier services to them; Cato, of course, had ensured by his rhetoric and persistence that that trial took place. The niceties of returning obligations did not figure in Clodius' plans – except, of course, when they happened to suit him. More significantly, Clodius was a populist who sought to build his power base amongst his plebeian 'constituents'; the tribunate thus provided an ideal opportunity for Clodius to create a pressure bloc that would endure beyond his tenure of the tribunate itself and which would grow from simple voting power to intimidatory street violence with the armed gangs that he recruited. This will have recalled the worst days of the Sullan era, but also reflected the fact that the stakes were moving ever higher, insofar as Clodius knew that his own continued rise through the *cursus honorum* would arouse fear and hostility amongst men like Pompey, Crassus and Caesar, not to mention Cato and Cicero.

The three, therefore, needed men in office to parry any attacks on the legislation; Clodius might suffice, but they also had, as consuls for 58, Caesar's father-in-law, Lucius Piso, and Pompey's old friend, Aulus Gabinius. It may be that in this atmosphere of uncertainty we may find a context for one of the more 'shadowy' episodes of the period – the so-called 'Vettius affair': it was alleged by Vettius, an informer, that a number of senators were plotting against Pompey's life; as we have seen, Pompey was extremely susceptible to this kind of rumour. It is possible that the affair was engineered by Caesar to dissuade Pompey from considering any kind of *rapprochement* with the senate during his absence from Rome. Alternatively, Clodius may have been the instigator, with the intention of preventing Pompey, who was still the most influential figure in Roman politics, from coming to the aid of men like Cicero and others whom he (Clodius) wished to attack. Ultimately, the question of whether there really was a plot against Pompey pales into insignificance against the question of who was responsible for the rumour. One effect of the episode was, predictably, to heighten Pompey's fear of assassination.

At the opening of the tribunician year, Clodius lost little time in putting before the *concilium plebis* a group of measures which had the collective aim of building his popularity and protecting him from attack. The introduction of a free grain handout to all citizens won him much support, as well as proving so costly that it threatened to deprive other projects of funds; this may have included the land commission set up under Caesar's land bills of 59. Clodius' legalisation of trades guilds, which had been outlawed by Cicero during his consulship, proved to be the means by which he could recruit his street gangs. At the same time, he restricted the powers of the censors to remove senators and outlawed the kind of religious manoeuvring that Bibulus had employed against Caesar in 59.

The intimidatory effect of the gangs was immediately apparent as Clodius proceeded against Cicero; outlawing those who had put Roman citizens to death without trial – of which, of course, Cicero had been guilty in his handling of the Catilinarians – was a neat way of encompassing the ruin of a man on whom he wished to have his revenge. It might also dissuade anyone from attempting to employ similar tactics against Clodius himself. Cicero was exiled and, in a move that was to cause the orator considerable difficulty later, Clodius had Cicero's house demolished and the site consecrated as a shrine to *libertas* ('freedom from tyranny'; 'freedom of Roman citizens not to be executed without trial').

Clodius moved in a more subtle fashion against Marcus Cato. Like Sulla, Cato had long been opposed to provincial appointments of an extraordinary nature – whether because of their length or because they were awarded to men whose progress through the *cursus honorum* did not justify them. Rome had recently acquired the island of Cyprus as a province; it needed to be organised and Clodius proposed that Cato, who had so far risen only to the rank of quaestor, should be given extraordinarily the standing of an ex-praetor to 'qualify' him for the responsibility. From Clodius' point of view, a vocal opponent was thus removed from Rome – and compromised: even Caesar appears to have appreciated the subtlety of this.

There was nothing subtle, however, about Clodius' treatment of Pompey; he was subject to attacks and humiliation by Clodius' gangs – to the extent that Pompey shut himself in his house for a good deal of 58 and hired gangs to counter those of Clodius: Pompey's 'gangleaders' were Publius Sestius and Titus Annius Milo, neither of whom could reasonably be described as anything other than disreputable characters. Clodius' motive in all of this was partly revenge, but partly to destroy Pompey's credibility and popularity and to prevent Pompey from taking active steps to secure the freedom of Cicero. This was Clodius working to secure ends of his own; much discussion has taken place on the question of which of Pompey's two partners might have been the inspiration for Clodius' attacks on Pompey. It must surely be the case, however, that neither Crassus nor Caesar would have wished to see Pompey humiliated to the point where he might seriously start reconsidering his friendships and alliances.

Moves to effect Cicero's restoration from exile began almost immediately; however, because of the hooliganism and corruption that were by now prevalent features of Roman politics, it took until August of 57 to secure the necessary legislation. This was due partly to intimidation by Clodius, but partly also to the fact that, whilst the three had not *actively* wished to have Cicero treated as Clodius had done (Caesar had even tried to save him from it), they were prepared to use the opportunity to place strict conditions on Cicero's activities in return for their support in the moves to restore him. Pompey, as we have seen, was virtually a prisoner in his own house because of Clodius' intimidation, and was probably coming to feel the loss of Cicero's support; he was probably also aware that his failure to do anything positive to help Cicero when Clodius was attacking him had done nothing to improve his standing in the eyes of leading senators.

Cicero returned in triumph – and to two interrelated issues: first, there was a shortage of corn (caused to a large extent by Clodius' reform of the dole in 58); and second, the pro-Roman (and pro-Pompeian) Ptolemy Auletes had been driven from the Egyptian throne. Egypt was the key to the grain supply and, as we have seen before, its wealth was much coveted by Roman politicians, who viewed it as a great aid to their ability to patronise. There is little doubt that Pompey wished to be entrusted with sorting out both of these problems, and it is equally clear that others wished to avoid giving Pompey sweeping new powers. Cicero's natural inclination, now reinforced by his sense of gratitude over Pompey's part in his restoration, was to support Pompey. But he had to be both diplomatic and cautious, for he needed the continuing goodwill of those senators, who held priesthoods and who were not necessarily well-disposed towards Pompey, in the matter of seeking the deconsecration of the shrine that Clodius had had erected on the site of Cicero's demolished house.

In the event, Cicero lent his support to a consular motion which gave Pompey control over the corn supply, but with powers far less wide than were proposed by Gaius Messius, one of the tribunes of 57, who was widely believed to be Pompey's mouthpiece. The question of the restoration of Auletes generated much more difficulty and ill-feeling; the matter, as Cicero shows in one of his liveliest letters, became the subject of raucous counter-chanting between gangs, which must have served to enhance Pompey's sense of humiliation. Cicero, too, found himself in something of a quandary because, whilst he wished to be support-ive of Pompey, one of Pompey's 'rivals' for the task was Publius Lentulus Spinther, one of the consuls of 57, who had himself been of great help in the matter of Cicero's restoration. In the end, this matter was dropped for the moment, and Aulus Gabinius, as proconsul of Syria, later took it on his own responsibility to effect Auletes' restoration.

During the following winter (57/56), Cicero was convinced that relations between Pompey, Caesar and Crassus, and the unpopular-ity of the three men, had developed to such an extent that they would cease supporting each other; he presumably entertained the hope that in these circumstances Pompey might come to realise where his best interests lay. Ever since 59, voices had been raised questioning the validity of Caesar's consular legislation; in the years that had followed, anti-Caesarian feeling in the senate will have grown amongst those who undoubtedly viewed with some apprehension not only Caesar's successes in Gaul but also the ruth-lessness of which he had shown himself to be capable. Lucius Domitius Ahenobarbus, one of the consular candidates for 55, made it known that, if elected, he would move for Caesar's recall from Gaul to face charges which would have effectively destroyed his career. In his enthusiasm for detaching Pompey from Caesar, Cicero joined in – at least to the extent of supporting the sugges-tion that the validity of the *lex Campana* should be questioned; Pompey, ever a master of dissimulation and obfuscation, indicated that he would not be averse to such a course of action.

Cicero probably misread the signs: for although Pompey's motives are not entirely clear, it seems likely that his 'threat' was designed not to complete Caesar's discomfiture but to demonstrate to him that he (Pompey) remained the major influence in the republic's politics and that Caesar still needed him. In other words, Pompey wished to remain in alliance with Caesar – but on his own terms.

The details of what happened as a result of this manoeuvring are unclear in the accounts of Plutarch and Appian; it is safest to say that meetings between the three men took place, perhaps at Lucca in northern Italy, and that out of them came a renewed private arrangement for mutual co-operation, though with the general purposes of achieving a visible balance between the actual powers of the three and of emasculating opposition. Each of the three emerged with military powers: Caesar's in Gaul were renewed for a further quinquennium, although – and this creates problems in our understanding of the final slide to civil war in 49 – it is not clear from when the new quinquennium was to run. The options are that either the new appointment ran on from the terminal date expressed in the *lex Vatinia* of 59 – that is, from 1 March 54 – or, alternatively, it may have run from a date in 55, perhaps coinciding with the granting of five-year commands to Pompey and Crassus in Spain and Syria respectively. Cicero, appalled by these developments, complained bitterly about the current state of affairs and men's untrustworthiness, but had little option but to stomach what had happened. In addition, the activities of Cicero and Clodius, which were seen as 'wrecking', were now to be reined in, so that opposition would lack coherence and leadership, both verbal and physical. Finally, Pompey and Crassus were to be joint consuls for 55; even so, Ahenobarbus continued to campaign until driven from the hustings by force early in 55. It is a mark of the upheaval and corruption of the elections that, despite having been due in the summer of 56, they had still not been run at the beginning of 55.

Although the *amicitia* was no more an instrument of government than it had been in 59, the situation in Rome following the new arrangements of 56/55 was very different: now, the three partners had extended commands with armies attached; Pompey and Crassus were consuls for 55; one of the three, Pompey, had obtained a dispensation to exercise his Spanish command through his *legati* and remain in Rome. It does not stretch the reality to argue that Pompey had emerged from the troubles of 58–56 with his hand greatly – if temporarily – strengthened.

The new stability was, however, short-lived. Caesar's second quinquennium in Gaul, which started with the expeditions to Britain in 55 and 54 and which brought Caesar much publicity in Rome, was marked in general by hard-won progress and by the dangerous rising of 52 under the talented Gallic leader Vercingetorix, which may in fact have received some support from Caesar's enemies in Rome. In 54 Julia, Pompey's wife and Caesar's daughter, died: the loss of Julia herself and her influence, not to mention that of the baby to whom she gave birth, decisively weakened the link between Pompey and Caesar. Pompey refused Caesar's offer to renew the marriage tie. Finally, in 53, Crassus, whose military experience since the 70s had been very limited, proved no match for the Parthians in the east and he was killed at Carrhae, losing a number of legionary standards ('eagles') as well; these were eventually recovered by the emperor Augustus.

Pompey, evidently confident of his dominance in Rome, continued to behave in a rather equivocal manner towards Caesar and, although doing nothing that would risk an open breach, was already setting about consolidating a position independent of his 'partner': in 52, for example, having declined Caesar's offer of a renewed marriage alliance, Pompey married Cornelia, the daughter of the senior senator Quintus Metellus Scipio. This sign of a *rapprochement* with senatorial leaders was no accident: both Pompey himself and Caesar's opponents in the senate were coming to see it as their most effective bulwark against the proconsul of Gaul. However, like many such arrangements, it was based more on a mutual and shared mistrust than on affection or a common philosophy. Further, for Pompey, his marriage to Cornelia had positive attractions beyond the status of her father: she was also the widow of Publius Crassus, who had been killed along with his father at Carrhae. There might be new connections to be had with a woman whose late husband had ties not only with his father's army but also, because the young Crassus had served for a time in Gaul, with Caesar's too. If there was anything of the truth in this, the cynicism of the move was not unworthy of Pompey.

Political violence in Rome reached new heights at the opening of 52: no magistrates whatever had been elected for the year, and in January, Publius Clodius, a candidate for the praetorship, was murdered in a gang fight with Milo, who had been Clodius' rival 'gangmaster' throughout the 50s and one-time 'protector' of Pompey. Amidst the turmoil, a dictatorship for Pompey was mooted and, as usual, the more that Pompey said that he did not want this the more people believed that he really did. However, with the support of Bibulus and Cato, Pompey was made sole consul; the senate had already passed the *senatus consultum ultimum*, giving Pompey special powers to restore order. Pompey's third consulship, in which in mid-year he took his new father-in-law, Metellus Scipio, as his colleague, was marked by a great deal of legislation that was of significance in the events leading up to the outbreak of civil war in 49.

Retroactive laws on violence and corruption were passed, and Milo was brought to court on a charge of having murdered Clodius. Pompey was by now hostile to Milo, whilst Cicero tried to defend him but 'broke down' under the intimidation of Milo's enemies; Cicero's surviving speech in Milo's defence is one that he 'worked up' for publication later. With his eyes on the future, Pompey sponsored all ten tribunes of 52 in passing a measure granting Caesar a dispensation from the normal rules governing personal presentation of candidature for office with which, of course, Caesar had encountered difficulties in 60. The 'law of the ten tribunes' was designed to allow Caesar to pass straight from his proconsulship to a second consulship (perhaps in 48). This would remove a period as a private citizen during which he would be liable for prosecution for past actions should anyone choose to pursue such a course. Cicero was later firmly of the view that this effectively precipitated civil war because it gave Caesar a clear privilege, which Pompey later tried to deny. Again, Pompey clouded the issue by bringing in a further law which insisted upon personal candidature, although he evidently later added a codicil to it which stated that this did not affect Caesar's rights under the law of the ten tribunes.

However, the law which was to cause all the difficulty and confusion in the negotiations between Caesar and Pompey during 51 and 50 was the *lex Pompeia de provinciis*. The principal aim of this law was to attack corruption by interposing an interval of five years between the tenure of the consulship and the taking up of a subsequent proconsulship; it was believed that the wealthy would be less ready to finance electoral corruption if they had to wait in excess of five years for a 'return' on their investments. The interval that had to elapse before the new rules were fully operational was to be filled by giving promagistracies to those who, like Cicero, had failed to take them at the proper time. Pompey's law, therefore, superseded that of Gaius Gracchus, which had enacted that the proconsular provinces should be determined in advance of the relevant elections. When the provincial arrangements of the three were agreed, Gaius Gracchus' law would have governed the timing of their supersession; since it is clear that there was to be no discussion of Caesar's supersession until 1 March 50, it would have been impossible to provide him with a successor earlier than one of the consuls of 49. Thus, it must have been anticipated, perhaps even agreed, in 56/55 that in practice Caesar would stay in Gaul until the end of 49, and that on 1 January 48 he would enter his second consulship. Now, under Pompey's new law, Caesar could be succeeded almost immediately after his term of office had formally expired, probably on 1 March 50.

It was a situation requiring, if conflict was to be avoided, a great store of goodwill between Caesar and Pompey; by 51 that commodity was diminishing rapidly. A final measure of Pompey's consular year was the securing of an extension of his own Spanish command; therefore, the certainty of his own continued armed protection contrasted strongly with the parlous predicament in which Caesar might conceivably find himself, particularly if his enemies were in the ascendant; they had evidently settled upon a 'battle plan', which looked more necessary after Caesar's crushing of Vercingetorix had crowned his Gallic campaigns with success. They could use their growing proximity to Pompey to destroy the 'common enemy', Caesar, and then abandon Pompey who, they appear to have imagined, would have been lost without his former partner. The cynicism of this at least matched Pompey's.

Throughout 51, Caesar's opponents in the senate, with more political ambition than good sense, sought to raise the political temperature; an attempt by one of the consuls, Marcus Claudius Marcellus, to have Caesar recalled in view of the fact that the

Gallic War was over, however, met with a frosty response from Pompey and a tribunician veto. Nor did the same consul encounter much sympathy when he ordered the flogging of a man from Comum (modern Como). A point at issue was that Caesar had settled a *colonia* of Roman citizens at Comum, and Marcellus was employing this ruse as a dramatic way of demonstrating that he did not regard Caesar's move as having validity; it may also have had the more serious intention of reflecting the disquiet felt at the fact that, well before the outbreak of hostilities at the beginning of 49, Caesar was concentrating troops in Cisalpine Gaul, something that it was much safer to do, now that the Gallic conflict was over.

In September of 51 Pompey met Caesar, and returned saying that there should be no discussion of Caesar's position until 1 March 50, but that after that date 'he would not hesitate'. Our source for this meeting and for many other of the crucial moments in the weeks and months leading to civil war is a letter written to Cicero by Marcus Caelius Rufus, one of a number which passed between the two men whilst Cicero was away from Rome as proconsul of Cilicia (51–50), a post which he had to take as a result of Pompey's law on the provinces and which Cicero himself regarded as tantamount to a second exile. Caelius was an astute observer of the political scene who served as Cicero's 'eyes and ears', although the precise significance of some of his observations are (for us, at least) difficult to interpret. In these letters we see Pompey as the source of responses which, on the face of things at any rate, appear to have been conciliatory to Caesar, but which lacked substance; for example, the 'compromise' proposal that Caesar should disarm on 13 November which would have meant a closing of the gap between leaving the proconsulship and entering the second consulship, but one which would have been useless to Caesar for it still left him with a period exposed as a *privatus*. The nub of the matter was that Caesar could not feel safe in leaving his province without his army, whilst Pompey could not feel safe as long as Caesar kept his army. Without some measure of willingness to trust, there could be no bridging of this gap.

Caesar's corner in Rome was defended through 50 by one of the tribunes, Gaius Scribonius Curio who, on his election to his office, suddenly changed his side to Caesar's. Curio persisted throughout the year, though to no avail, in attempting to interpose his veto against attempts to dispossess Caesar of his provinces and army. Cicero returned from Cilicia in November and saw, as he himself remarked in frustration, that he had entered a 'madhouse of men thirsting for war'. And so it seemed, although the 'warmongers' were in fact a small, but vocal and influential, minority, as was demonstrated when on 1 December Curio called for a vote on his proposal that Pompey and Caesar should surrender their provinces simultaneously; the senate passed this by 370 votes to 22, but the vote was immediately vetoed by a tribune acting for the 22. At this, Gaius Claudius Marcellus, one of the consuls for 50, called upon Pompey to save the republic.

Pompey's acceptance was the penultimate step before civil war; on 1 January, two of the new tribunes of 49, Antonius and Cassius, re-presented Curio's disarmament proposal, but this was countered by a move to declare Caesar a 'public enemy' (*hostis*). Antonius and Cassius were 'advised' to leave Rome, and the senate, despite its earlier expression of a desire for peace, passed the *senatus consultum ultimum*. Caesar now felt that he was left with no alternative; with his army he crossed the river Rubicon, the stream that separated his province from Italy, and so the civil war had begun. Caesar, ever the populist, could argue that he was fighting for the traditional rights of the tribunes – the ten who, in 52, had granted him his dispensation, and the two (Antonius and Cassius) whose veto had recently been set aside. Ultimately, Caesar argued that he was fighting for his status (*dignitas*) and the integrity of his career. Caesar was always the man to try and make his enemies appear unreasonable: on this occasion, he could argue that it was they who had forced him to fight; as he observed later, the civil war was their wish.

Caesar's enemies made out that they had gone to war to save the republic from the domination of individuals; many Romans, such as Cicero, agonised over which side they should join; indeed, in a jaundiced moment Cicero recognised that it made little difference since both leaders 'wanted to be king'. The war divided friends and families: Cicero, after some four months of deliberation, joined Pompey and the senate, and persuaded his brother, Quintus, to do the same. However, Cicero's friend, Caelius Rufus, joined Caesar. Cicero soon came to see that there was little honour in the 'Pompeian cause': many of the leading senators on Pompey's side were narrow-minded bigots, men deep in debt, who regarded the republic as their own preserve for the pursuance of their ancestral ambitions, and men who looked on civil war as providing an opportunity for personal enrichment as they anticipated the spoils which would fall to them in the aftermath of their victory. From the republic's point of view, this tragedy was compounded by the fact that those on Caesar's side were little different.

The war went on in various theatres of the empire until 45, but the decisive battle was fought at Pharsalus in Greece in 48. Pompey and his followers had quit Italy early in 49, not so much to save the homeland from the ravages of civil war as to establish their bases within striking distance of the wealth and clientage waiting in Asia Minor; Pompey hoped that this would win the war for him, as well as stretching Caesar's lines of communication and supply. Pompey was beaten at Pharsalus; it was said that some 30,000 of his men died there, although the figure is disputed. Pompey himself escaped to Egypt, seeking refuge with the son of Ptolemy Auletes. However, the young Ptolemy and his sister Cleopatra were more concerned to propitiate the rising than the setting sun; to this end they had Pompey murdered – an abject end for a man who, despite a political performance that often seemed uncongenial and duplicitous, had achieved much for Rome and her empire.

For Caesar and those who survived, there was little space, or indeed inclination, for triumphalism; the priorities were now reconciliation and an attempt to reconstruct the shattered republic.

# 6

## THE DICTATORSHIP OF JULIUS CAESAR

The civil war provided no answer to the republic's problems in itself; as we have seen, it split families and friends apart as they tried to weigh the rights and wrongs, the advantages and disadvantages of the two sides. It was a measure of the personal torment caused by this that when Quintus Cicero sought Caesar's 'pardon' for having joined Pompey's side he roundly blamed his brother, Marcus, for his 'error'. In contrast, Cicero's friend, Caelius Rufus, chose Caesar's side because he thought that Caesar would win; Cicero himself, although he had developed an increasing personal affection for Caesar in the later 50s – not least because of the fact that, on one occasion, Caesar had put himself in danger to save Cicero's brother, Quintus – eventually joined Pompey out of loyalty and because, for him, Pompey's alliance with the senate seemed to offer hope that it was the 'better side'. However, Cicero soon discovered, as Syme observed in *The Roman Revolution*, that, whilst 'liberty' and 'the republic' were high-sounding words, in practice they meant little more than the maintenance of the privileges and vested interests of the nobility.

Caesar's supporters in the civil war were a disparate group: his army; the urban plebeians; equestrians; patrician families, long-depressed politically and financially, who saw in Caesar's rise an opportunity to better themselves; and senators, particularly younger members, who felt alienated by the behaviour of their seniors. Some of Caesar's supporters were plain adventurers, whilst others joined him out of a personal attachment; we should not lose sight of the fact that although Caesar could be extremely harsh to his enemies and intolerant of opposition there was a degree of personal loyalty and magnetism in him which con-trasted with the cynical behaviour of many of those involved in the civil war.

A major problem for Caesar, however, was that, whilst such a disparate group as his was relatively easy to hold together during the short space of the civil war, the breadth of its expectations inevitably made this much harder in peacetime. Another serious difficulty for Caesar when he set out for war, but even more so as he embarked upon post-war reconstruction, was caused by the fact that the great luminaries of the republic, the noble families, had generally joined Pompey. This inevitably made Caesar stand out above his supporters in a way that many came to see as increas-ingly 'monarchic'; Caesar himself was sensitive about this, as is seen in his famous response that he was 'not king, but Caesar'.

A further difficulty which affected Caesar was that, whilst he won the decisive victory of the civil war at Pharsalus in 48, many of Pompey's supporters vowed to continue fighting and, under the command of Pompey's sons, carried the war on until 45. The fact, therefore, that Caesar was not free from war until so late was bound to affect his attitude to the whole political landscape. Yet if he was to heal the republic he had to be ready to come to terms with those defeated enemies who made overtures to him; it was certainly not Caesar's intention to deal with opposition in the way that Sulla had done in 81 and 80. By contrast, Caesar made a virtue of the conciliatory attitude which he displayed to those who had opposed him by publicising his *clementia* ('clemency'). This was not weakness or softness on Caesar's part, however; he knew that if he was to succeed in restoring peace and stability he would have to carry with him a good proportion of his defeated enemies. Yet even his *clementia* carried political risks; not only was there a danger for Caesar in surrounding himself with new associates, such as Marcus Brutus, whom it might ultimately prove rash to have trusted, but also, as Cassius was to observe in a letter to Cicero in 45, *clementia* was itself a 'virtue' associated with *dominatio*: its application did not depend upon rights and laws but on the victor's whim; it could, therefore, be withdrawn as easily and as arbitrarily as it was granted.

Caesar knew that it was not sufficient merely to hope that, after the war, the peace would look after itself; it seems that he may have been a man who gave thought to the needs of government, and his thinking did not remain simply on the theoretical level. He gave active consideration to the methods by which Rome and Italy could sit at the centre of a well-ordered, well-defended and prosperous empire. He had already indicated his interest in such matters with a new law on extortion passed during his first consulship in 59 and, more recently, with his relatively liberal treatment of defeated Gauls, leaving them free of the ravages of Roman tax collectors by introducing the concepts of tax assessment and local responsibility for collection. He also put before them the opportunities inherent in grants of Roman citizenship. In effect, this was the *pax Romana* of Augustus in its infancy.

It may also be surmised that Caesar recognised some of the problems of Rome's domestic politics; in particular, it must have been obvious to him that the republic was becoming increasingly ungovernable as individuals and groups promoted themselves using the opportunities of wealth and military power which the growing empire had brought in its wake. 'The republic', Caesar is reported to have observed, 'is a mere name, without form or substance.' This could, of course, simply have been the contemptuous remark that it is often taken to have been, signalling that he felt free to do whatever he wished; equally, it might have meant that, in his view, there was nothing 'sacred' in the way that the government had been carried out in the early days; just as the republic's institutions had evolved to meet changing needs in the past, so they should be able to continue to do in the present and the future.

Thus, Caesar may have begun to contemplate how he could preserve as much as possible of the republic's governmental traditions, whilst providing them with the means to achieve stability; in this he was perhaps adumbrating the course of action to be followed by his adopted son, Augustus. As we have seen, Cicero, too, had thought along such lines, hoping that the *consensus bonorum*, which he felt that he had established in 63, might be retained on a more permanent footing, and strengthened. His

'Union of the Orders', under the benevolent guidance of a man of *auctoritas*, whom he called the *moderator*, was his preferred solution, although the outbreak of the civil war had shown how great were the problems that stood in the way of the fulfilment of such hopes. If the civil war had shown anything at all, it was that 'union' of any kind was a singularly inappropriate word to apply to the Roman republic of the mid-first century. One of Cicero's difficulties was his tendency – certainly evidenced in his 'crusades' against Catiline and, later, Antonius – to confuse symptoms and causes. Because of this, he came to believe that 'solutions' which derived from specific events might have a more general application. Cicero, of course, had until the civil war identified Pompey with his *moderator*; there is some evidence to suggest that, by 47–46, he was coming to hope that Caesar might be persuaded to take this role. Whether Caesar had ever given Cicero any reason for such hopes is another matter.

Caesar's task was to put the republic in order, and heal the wounds of recent years; to do this he had to find the means of making his approaches acceptable. Some might follow Caesar without question: an example is Gaius Matius who communicated his feelings to Cicero after Caesar's assassination. However, convincing defeated enemies, and even reluctant friends, was another matter. Many of those who returned to Rome after Pharsalus were sufficiently eager for peace to contemplate the necessity of temporary supervision of the republic by Caesar, at least until bruised sensibilities began to heal. Cicero was amongst these, and he might have gone further had events not demonstrated to him that Caesar's supervision represented a slippery slope to autocracy.

Although Caesar may have wished to provide a new start for the republic, a phoenix rising from the ashes of civil war, control and setting himself above potential rivals appear to have been uppermost in his political thinking: his observation that Sulla simply demonstrated his political foolishness when he resigned his dictatorship seems to point to this. Thus, from the start, Caesar's control was emphasised: the basis of it was the dictatorship which he held for varying periods from 49, and which became 'perpetual' in 44. It is, however, important to make the point that by this latter move Caesar was not necessarily becoming dictator for ever, but rather that he was holding the office for an *indefinite* period without the statement of a terminal date when, in compliance with republican tradition, he could be called to account for his tenure. This may represent poor judgement on Caesar's part, but it also shows his view that the supervision that the republic required – and indeed his own need for personal political protection – stretched into a longer-term future. The great advantages that the dictatorship held for him were that the *imperium* of the office was 'superior' to that of other magistracies and, because the traditions of the office were rooted in national emergencies, it carried immunity from the tribunician veto.

Caesar was also consul in 48 and from 46 to 44; indeed, in 45 he was sole consul, as Pompey had been in 52. What he intended to convey or achieve by this plurality and iteration of offices remains unclear: did he intend, by his holding of the consulship, to bring the appearance of 'republican normality' to his activities or was he trying to restrict the openings available to other members of the nobility? It is said that he even contemplated following the example of Publius Clodius in seeking a *transitio ad plebem* so that he could hold the office of tribunate of the plebeians; there is little real evidence to support this contention, although in 44 he was given a special grant of tribunician inviolability (*sacrosanctitas*). Since 63, Caesar had been chief priest (*pontifex maximus*), the 'chairman' of all of the republic's priesthoods, and in 47 he became an *augur*: these offices provided Caesar with a strong control over the religious activity of the republic, with all the opportunities for political manoeuvring that attached to the state religion. It is clear, too, that Caesar enjoyed certain censorial powers – over the senate's membership and over the republic's moral and social fabric. In all, these powers and positions, in addition to his military pre-eminence and patronage, meant that he exercised a dominant role over the government of the republic.

Does the extent of his powers, however, provide us with an idea of Caesar's view of the republic or does it simply point to the way in which he saw his position *at the time*? How did all of this leave the traditional organs of the republic's government? The popular assemblies were on their way to becoming ciphers; Caesar's widespread powers and patronage of equestrians, urban plebeians and armies saw to this. The senate, too, changed its role and appearance: Caesar removed from it responsibility for finance and foreign policy which, in any case, it had usurped from the people; further, whilst stories of Caesar's wish to fill the senate with 'trousered Gauls' were clearly exaggerated, his view of the senate to some degree at least broke with the past, perhaps emphasising its consultative role. But was he trying, as was the emperor Claudius later, to make the senate more representative of Italy and the growing empire rather than of Rome alone? Whilst this is possible and may indeed carry part of the truth, we must remember that, like any victorious leader, Caesar had supporters who were looking for rewards in terms of status and whose continued loyalty had to be guaranteed. The problem was that, with the senate's membership increased to around 900 – mainly made up with Caesar's supporters – it was likely, perhaps inevitable, that the dictator should come to treat the body as a mere 'rubber stamp'. However, this could be – and was – carried to disturbing lengths: Cicero complained of an occasion when he found his name added to the list of signatories to a senatorial decree, although he had not even been present at the meeting concerned.

Caesar's attitude to the magistracies was equally cavalier: he did not abolish elections, but the extent of his patronage ensured that they became more of a formality. The numbers of annual magistrates were increased both to reward supporters and to ensure a sufficient supply of men for the jobs involved. On some occasions, however (for example, in 47 and 45), regular officers were not elected and administrative affairs were handed temporarily to 'prefects' (*praefecti*) of Caesar's choosing. There is no doubt that all of this was seen by many as a serious departure from traditional arrangements and an elimination of traditional opportunities (*libertas*). Caesar had long had a tendency to be intolerant of opposition, regarding it as unreasonable, but his treatment of the instruments of government was bound to heighten opposition rather than allay it. It is hardly surprising in these circumstances that, in 46, a man as tenacious in his regard for tradition as was Marcus Cato should prefer suicide to life in Caesar's republic.

Much that Caesar did or planned was directed, at least in part, towards achieving a harmonious empire with Rome at its centre, an imperial city worthy of the name. Attention was given to improving the financial and governmental position of the provinces over the empire as a whole along the lines that he had adumbrated in Gaul. Colonies of his veterans and of other citizens from Rome were planted across the empire to enhance stability and security – Caesar's own as well as Rome's. Measures such as these enhanced trade and, in this way, gave local people the opportunity to prosper and thus qualify through wealth for local administrative office; the treasury in Rome would in its turn benefit from an improved tax-take. There was much in this that was taken on by the emperors who came after Caesar and developed by them.

The question, however, that inevitably arises out of a consideration of Caesar's short period in power is whether he was aiming at a form of monarchy; Caesar was not unnaturally sensitive to such criticism, and it has even been suggested that he consciously 'went over the top' so that he could then deny strenuously any idea of monarchic intentions. Caesar's behaviour appears to some historians – and was seen by some contemporaries – to have been becoming more autocratic and arbitrary: his attitude and the appearance of his image on the coinage seem to point in that direction. So, too, the swearing of an oath of allegiance to him, his adoption of 'monarchic' dress, and the placing of his statue on the Capitolium, where he removed the inscription commemorating the rebuilding by Quintus Lutatius Catulus and substituted his own name. Then, there was the outrageous splendour of his triumphs, which after all were mostly 'earned' in civil strife not against foreign enemies.

We should also take into account his inauguration of a substantial building programme – a public hall adjacent to the Forum (*Basilica Iulia*), a new public square and 'business park' (*Forum Iulium*) – which was put into action; alongside it were plans to relieve the flooding of the river Tiber, the improvement of road maintenance, the draining of the Pomptine Marshes and the reconstruction of Rome's harbour at Ostia. Such projects may have been conceived as a way of elevating Caesar's image, although it cannot be denied that all of these were useful and necessary, and all of them provided ordinary people with work so that they could afford their own food rather than having to rely on state handouts; it should not be overlooked that the number of those in receipt of the corn dole was reduced by around one-half. Again, the initiation of a building programme which had more than a single purpose looks forward to future bearers of the name 'Caesar'. The 'bills' for such work could be paid from the spoils of Caesar's wars; no doubt, too, his association with Cleopatra opened his eyes to the availability of Egyptian wealth.

That Caesar, from the mid-40s, was coming to dominate Rome cannot be easily denied: the manner of Cleopatra's introduction into Rome, for example, was hardly traditional, nor the way in which her golden statue was placed in the great temple to Venus Genetrix ('Venus the Founder' – that is, of Rome and of the Julian family), which was the 'crowning glory' of the *Forum Iulium*. This was a presumptuous insult to the members of Rome's nobility who also looked back to mythological, sometimes divine, origins. Such a 'promotion' of the Egyptian queen must for many have been a tasteless demonstration of how far Julius Caesar had strayed from the path of tradition. Even so, there is no evidence that Caesar wished to live with Cleopatra, nor that he wanted to move the capital of the empire to Alexandria or rule after the fashion of a Hellenistic monarch or bequeath his 'kingdom' to Caesarion, his and Cleopatra's son.

So what did all of this signify? Did Caesar have pretensions to divinity himself? It is true that in the east cults of his divinity were recognised, although, as with the emperors, this probably represented no more than the adoption of a 'local mechanism' for demonstrating elevated and commanding status. Despite contemporary gossip, there is no evidence of the actual existence of a cult of 'Jupiter Julius', and statues of Caesar were more likely intended as exaggerated objects of honour rather than of worship. Caesar, it can reasonably be said, was not deified until after his death.

The autocrat of 46 to 44 seems very distant from the conqueror of Gaul and the man who negotiated with Pompey before the outbreak of the civil war; yet for some the arrogance that he was already showing was a pointer to what might happen. The suicide of Cato in 46 was in a sense a defining moment; although Caesar and Cato had never seen eye to eye, Cato's 'final statement' was an altogether harsher judgement of his long-term adversary. The suicide must also have given many others pause for thought, particularly as they surveyed life in Caesar's republic: in a sense, it mattered little whether he actually called himself a king or a god; the scant regard in which Caesar appeared to hold the republic's institutions was sufficient to show that he was a tyrant.

It is possible that by 46–45 Caesar was coming to appreciate that he had no real answer to the republic's problems – at least, not one that was broadly acceptable. Matius' letter to Cicero made the point that 'Caesar could not find a way out', and it has been suggested that the campaigns on the Danube and in the east which Caesar was planning at the time of his death convey a sense of escapism – or possibly he hoped that they would give him the opportunity to enhance his military reputation.

Cato's death was followed by the publication of eulogistic pamphlets about him; Caesar, rather unwisely, insisted on producing his own *Anti-Cato*, which was counterproductive in that, if anything, it heightened the perception of antithesis between the two men, which was evidently still momentous three years later when the historian Sallust wrote his account of the Catilinarian conspiracy of 63. The climax of Sallust's work was the debate on the fate of the conspirators, in which 'pride of place' was given to the orations of Caesar and Cato. These orations, especially Cato's, are very clearly products of their times.

Caesar was evidently aware of his growing unpopularity and sensitive to the campaign of disinformation that was, during 45 and 44, being mounted against him; the purpose of this was presumably to isolate the dictator and to justify taking action against him. Caesar seemed particularly concerned at the growing disenchantment that he noticed in Cicero, a man whom, in a sense, Caesar saw as a kind of 'national barometer': Cicero had joined Caesar after the civil war because, although he felt that the republic needed, temporarily at least, Caesar's kind of authority, he was clear in his mind that after a while Caesar should be able to resign his overarching powers. This, of course, had not happened, and Cicero himself was deeply dejected – depressed over the 'abolition' of the republic and, in addition, suffering badly after the loss of his beloved daughter, Tullia; the 'old Caesar', the man of culture, grace and charm, was now rarely to be seen. It is hardly surprising that against this background some started to contemplate radical solutions, motivated by a combination of concerns for the future of the republic as well as, in some cases, by personal grievances. At all events, it was becoming increasingly obvious to some that Caesar, the author and beneficiary of *dominatio*, had to go.

February of 44 was clearly crucial; it was the month in which Caesar became *dictator perpetuus*, and it was also the month in which Antonius, now consul, orchestrated the incident of the offer and refusal of the golden diadem. Caesar was due to leave for his eastern campaign on 18 March, having fixed all appointments to domestic and provincial posts for the next two years, disregarding any republican formalities over such matters. As if to 'rub salt in the wound', Caesar effectively left his associates Oppius and Balbus in charge at Rome; anyone having business with Caesar during his absence would thus be required to approach him through two men who were not even senators.

The instigators of the plot to assassinate Caesar were Gaius Cassius Longinus and his brother-in-law Marcus Junius Brutus; both had supported Pompey until Pharsalus, but had then offered their services to Caesar. Cassius appears to have yielded leadership of the conspiracy to Brutus, a man who had entertained high hopes of Caesar (he was praetor in 44), but who was perhaps too deeply influenced by his descent from the Brutus who, according to tradition, had founded the republic and by his more immediate family connections with Cato and Bibulus. Of the twenty known names of conspirators, nine had fought with Pompey, seven with Caesar, whilst the remaining four had been with Caesar in Gaul. This mixture of immediate backgrounds reflects well the nature of Caesar's problem of trying to satisfy a variety of interests between 48 and 44, as well as his failure to find an acceptable solution.

The conspirators seem to have taken the view, rather like the Athenian tyrannicides in the late-sixth century BC, that the death of the tyrant himself would immediately lead to the recovery of constitutional integrity. Indeed, Antonius was to be left alive – an omission which Cicero later saw to have been a vital error, claiming that the 'banquet of the Ides of March had been one course short'. Further, the *libertas* for the sake of which Caesar was struck down, whilst of concern to members of the senatorial nobility, was of very little interest to the mass of the population – the people, the armies, the equestrians and even some senators – who were coming to feel that sense of dependence on the 'national leader' (*princeps*) that was to be a feature of the Augustan principate.

Caesar may not, in his final moments, have been too surprised to have been struck down by the assassin's knife, although he was, it seems, shocked that it was wielded by Brutus. There seems, however, little to support the contention that Caesar 'walked into' assassination as a kind of 'constructive suicide'.

With Caesar dead, the republic had no obvious leader, although Antonius, as consul in 44, was in the best position to seize the initiative – something that in the short term he was able to do, because Caesar's assassins had laid no positive plans beyond the single act of removing the tyrant; the republic thus remained as deeply in trouble as ever.

# 7

## THE FINAL ACT: ANTONIUS, OCTAVIAN AND LEPIDUS

As we have seen, the initiative, after Caesar's murder, did not long remain with the conspirators. Whilst they took refuge from popular anger, the surviving consul, Marcus Antonius, who, despite a frankly undistinguished early career, had been well enough regarded by Caesar to be treated as his 'deputy', took full advantage of the confusion to assert the continuing domination of the Caesarian faction with himself as its new leader; other Caesarians, such as Marcus Lepidus, were persuaded to support Antonius. Claiming to use Caesar's will, Antonius made himself the centre of patronage, offered some concessions to republican sentiment, including an amnesty for the conspirators in return for the survival of Caesar's legislative measures (*acta*), and thus claimed responsibility for the return of ordered government. He also ensured that after his consulship he would receive the lucrative province of Macedonia, thus inheriting the military plans that Caesar had laid in the east. Republicans, like Cicero, might rail at this, but with little political, and less military, muscle, there was little that they could do about it; Antonius had gambled, and apparently succeeded.

The difficulties of Caesar's deputy, however, emanated from a much less obvious source. In his last months, Caesar had adopted as his son and heir his great-nephew, Gaius Octavius, and enrolled the eighteen-year-old amongst the patricians. This obscure young man, whom Caesar had treated as a son for some years, thus became Gaius Julius Caesar Octavianus; although for clarity's sake we refer to him as Octavian, he disliked this part of his adoptive nomenclature and, for obvious reasons, preferred to style himself 'Caesar'.

When Julius Caesar was assassinated, Octavian was in the Balkans, waiting with his young friend Marcus Agrippa to join Caesar on his planned eastern expedition: it was intended to be the first step on an 'apprenticeship' that would in time lead them both to senatorial careers. Octavian was back in Italy by April; not surprisingly, he did not find Antonius particularly helpful. Caesar's deputy was bitter about the position of Caesar's heir and was clearly in no mood to treat him on equal terms. Nor, in one sense, was this unreasonable, since Antonius was consul and, according to Sulla's rules, Octavian should have expected to have to wait for nearly a quarter of a century more to reach that position. Unwisely, Antonius was dismissive, saying publicly that Octavian 'owed everything to his name', but at the same time he reorganised the proconsular provinces for 43 BC, giving up Macedonia (though retaining its army) and receiving instead a five-year command of Cisalpine and Transalpine Gaul. For republicans whom he was aiming to conciliate, this was a rash reminder of Caesar's position in the late 50s BC.

Caesar's friends and veterans, however, welcomed the new Caesar; some republicans, like Cicero, even began to see Octavian as an ally against Antonius, rather unwisely reviving the plan that Cato had originally inspired for playing off Pompey and Caesar against each other in the late 50s BC. Octavian was using his own resources to appeal to Caesar's veterans and even won over two of Antonius' legions; Cicero, for his part, was highly flattered that the 'divine youth' should choose to sit at his feet. With a new confidence, Cicero thundered out his series of 'Philippic orations' against Antonius, seeking at every turn to undermine the credibility of the man who was aiming at dictatorship and was more to be feared even than Julius Caesar. Even Brutus and Cassius, who were busy suborning the troops of pro-Antonius proconsuls in the east, became worried at the obsessive exclusiveness of Cicero's vituperations.

Cicero's plan was that at the end of 44 BC Antonius should be denied access to the province of which, however undesirable it might seem, he was the legally appointed *proconsul*; that the senate should support Decimus Brutus, Antonius' predecessor in that province and one of the conspirators against Caesar, in a refusal to give way; and that an army should be sent north to defeat Antonius, headed by Hirtius and Pansa, the consuls of 43 BC. Further, Octavian was to be given a special grant of propraetorian *imperium* to qualify him for a commanding role in this expedition. For the second time in his career, Cicero was proposing that the republic should set aside its laws to defeat an enemy in the name of some higher, and ill-defined, justice.

Antonius, who besieged Decimus Brutus at Mutina (modern Modena), was defeated, but escaped. In the event, it appears more than possible that this was allowed to happen by the collusive connivance of Lepidus and Octavian. In the fighting, the consuls had been killed, leaving Octavian as *de facto* commander of the republic's whole army. Instructed by Cicero and the senate to hand these troops over to the senior republican commander in the area (Decimus Brutus), Octavian refused, arguing now that he could not be expected to co-operate with a man who had had a hand in the assassination of his adoptive father; the 'divine youth' was already displaying a great maturity in political cynicism. Instead, he marched his eight legions on Rome, demanded (and received) a consulship from a senate that now presumably appreciated the gravity of its misjudgement, and straightaway returned north to meet Antonius and Lepidus.

The result of the meeting was the formation of the second triumvirate. This was not an informal, private arrangement after the manner of that between Pompey, Crassus and Caesar; rather, it was an organ of government, sanctified in law, with the task of stabilising the republic. Thus, the single dictator, assassinated on 15 March 44 BC, was on 27 November 43 BC replaced in effect (but not in title) by three. They divided the west between them, a division which by its nature clearly marked out Antonius as the senior partner and which left Octavian with the 'maritime' provinces of Africa, Sicily and Sardinia – which would be difficult to control in view of the piratical activities of Pompey's surviving son, Sextus, who was based on Sicily and styling himself in grandiose fashion the 'son of Neptune'. Despite the formal 'job description' of the triumvirate, the triple personality cult on the coinage, as well as the conduct of the three, made it abundantly clear that the restoration of the republic, for which Brutus and Cassius had assassinated Caesar, was dead.

The immediate task of the new triumvirate, which was made up of three men who ostensibly derived their political credentials from Julius Caesar, was to lead the Caesarian faction in avenging its dead leader's murder. To do this, they needed money to pay troops and settle veterans, and whilst away in the east they needed to have confidence in political stability in Rome and Italy. The solution to both necessities was the instigation of a new programme of proscriptions after the model introduced by Sulla; although the programme had some prominent victims, including (predictably) Cicero, the clear majority came from the equestrian order, indicating that money was the chief priority.

As a result, by the summer of 42 BC the three could put forty-three legions into the field to match the nineteen that Brutus and Cassius had acquired by fairly dubious means in the east, and which they maintained by the results of their rapacity in Asia Minor. The political heirs of Caesar had in effect to repeat what Caesar had himself had to do in 49/48 BC – take on with stretched supply lines an enemy that had considerable resources close at hand. The battles at Philippi in Greece proved conclusive: whilst Lepidus had been left to keep order in Italy, and Octavian was too sick to participate fully in the campaigns, Antonius first inflicted a defeat on Cassius which drove the latter to suicide and undermined the morale of Brutus' troops, who had had some initial success against Octavian. With Cassius gone, however, the defeat of Brutus was more easily secured; again the main impetus for victory was Antonius. Like Cassius before him, Brutus, seeing that no hope was left, committed suicide. Of their supporters, some joined the *triumviri*, whilst others, particularly those most implacably opposed to Caesarism, took refuge with Sextus Pompeius on Sicily. Thus, the avenging of Caesar's murder was complete, later to be symbolised by the construction in Rome of a temple to Mars the Avenger.

In the aftermath of Philippi, a new territorial division took place. Antonius received Gaul and the east, where it was intended that he would acquire funds for the settlement of veterans; Lepidus was at first given nothing, on the ground that he was aiding and abetting Sextus Pompeius, but was later to receive Africa; Octavian, who had since Caesar's deification been entitled to style himself *divi filius* ('son of god'), received Spain, Italy and the islands, as well as Africa. Without doubt, Octavian had been given the most difficult and dangerous post-war task, for he had to handle Sextus Pompeius and mastermind a huge programme of land confiscation, mainly in Italy, in order to discharge all but eleven of the triumviral legions. It is tolerably clear that Antonius had hoped and expected that his colleague would be fatally submerged in the unpopularity that would attend such a programme and, to make sure, had primed his wife and brother to exacerbate Octavian's problems.

Octavian survived all of this and defeated his opponents at the town of Perusia (modern Perugia), showing little mercy, but pardoning Antonius' brother. Octavian's successful surmounting of this crisis brought Antonius back to Italy and a new agreement, the treaty of Brundisium (40 BC). By this the earlier territorial division was adjusted, adding Gaul to Octavian's command and giving Africa to Lepidus; the agreement was sealed by a marriage between the recently widowed Antonius and Octavian's sister, Octavia. In a manner that looks forward to aspects of Augustan succession policy, it may have been hoped that a union between the deputy leader of Caesar's party and the family of Caesar's heir would itself produce an heir that would draw the whole Caesarian faction together – as when, some twenty years later, Augustus arranged a marriage between his friend Agrippa and his daughter Julia.

The ensuing decade, the last before the battle of Actium (31 BC) and the emergence of Octavian unrivalled in primacy, was dominated by the polarisation of the positions and support of Antonius and Octavian. Antonius was by now preoccupied with the problems of the east, including his relationship with Cleopatra, whilst Octavian, despite difficulties, consolidated his dominance of the west. This enabled him increasingly to present himself as the centre of a network of patronage for politicians, financiers and literary figures. The respectability that went with this enabled Octavian to begin to draw a veil across the excesses of the early triumviral years; it was a respectability that was enhanced by the fact that, as the members of his faction themselves grew in stature, he was able to emphasise the role of himself and his faction in stabilising peace, security and prosperity in the west. He was thus able increasingly to use his own well-developed demagogic skills and his control of propaganda to show that he was the defender, indeed the embodiment, of all that was best in Roman and Italian tradition.

By contrast, that same propaganda machine was able to mini-mise the undoubted successes of Antonius in the east, emphasise his difficulties (as when, in 36 BC, one of his generals, Decidius Saxa, lost further prestige to the Parthians), and play on the untraditional dalliance with Cleopatra, and the plans, real or sup-posed, that the two had for the future of the Roman world. Not only that, but Octavian, who had adequately shown in 44 and 43 BC the pliability of his principles, was able to stand as the moral paragon rebuking Antonius for defiling the honour of Octavia. Thus, events enabled Octavian to put the integrity of traditional Italian political and family life at the top of his programme.

There were, of course, difficulties along the way, though on more than one occasion Octavian displayed an adept skill at grab-bing success out of difficulty. For example, soon after the treaty of Brundisium, Sextus Pompeius, annoyed at having been ignored, increased his piratical activities. A new accord between him and the three, signed at Misenum (near Naples) in 39 BC, not only (temporarily at least) satisfied Sextus Pompeius but also allowed the large number of senatorial families whose loyalty to the repub-lic had led them to take refuge with the son of Pompey to return to Italy. Members of senior senatorial families, whose opposition to Julius Caesar had been intense, could now re-enter public life under the patronage of the new Caesar. This was important for it saved Octavian from the danger, which had proved so serious for Caesar, of being surrounded by men who socially (and thus politically) were of small account.

As if to symbolise his new understanding with the luminaries of the republic, Octavian, in circumstances which some thought scandalous, divorced his wife, Scribonia, and married Livia Drusilla, herself the wife of Tiberius Claudius Nero, an erstwhile supporter and latterly bitter opponent of Julius Caesar. Livia and Tiberius Nero already had one son (the future emperor Tiberius), and Livia was pregnant again at the time of her divorce and remarriage. She was recommended not just by the social respectability of her husband but also by the blood of the Livii Drusi and the patrician Claudii Pulchri that she carried in her veins.

Relations between Octavian and Sextus Pompeius did not improve for long, and in 37 BC, at Tarentum, the triumvirate, which had formally lapsed at the end of the previous year, was renewed for a further five years. The help that Octavian received from Antonius in the form of 120 ships enabled him, through the agency of Agrippa, now his senior commander, to take on Sextus Pompeius and defeat him in 36 BC. A bizarre, but dangerous attempt by Lepidus to reassert himself and claim Sicily was thwarted by Octavian's presenting himself to the troops as 'Caesar'; the name still served to inspire loyalty and obedience. Lepidus, for his trouble, was stripped of his triumviral title and left to live out his days as *pontifex maximus* in Africa.

The defeat of Sextus Pompeius was proclaimed as the establishment of peace; Octavian's generals, acting under the auspices of *imperator Caesar*, had defeated their enemies on land and at sea. As if themselves looking to the normalities of life in peacetime, the plebs granted to Octavian the personal inviolability of a tribune; like Caesar, of course, Octavian was a patrician and thus was ineligible to hold the office of tribune. Other signs of peace were in the air: the settlement of veteran colonies in Italy and the provinces, the beginnings of restoration of the temples of the traditional gods, and the physical enhancement of Rome and Italy with buildings intended for the purposes of entertainment and relaxation, promoting business life, and striking a suitable tone for a successful imperial city. All of this was viewed in Rome as being in marked contrast to the more equivocal record of Marcus Antonius. In particular, his 'Donations of Alexandria' in 34 BC made a bad impression; in these arrangements he divided the east between his and Cleopatra's children, proclaimed Cleopatra as 'queen of kings' and announced that Caesarion was Caesar's true heir, thus implying the illegitimacy of Octavian's claim to that title.

Octavian's propaganda machine was able to make much of this, but we may ask how outrageous it really was. Placing territory into the hands of friendly monarchs (client kings) was to become a regular feature of overseas policy under the emperors and had already been used to a certain extent in Rome's dealings with Asia Minor. At no time did Antonius claim for himself an eastern title, though he did attract many of the visible signs of eastern monarchy; he continued to justify his activities by his triumviral power, and coins issued in the east as late as 32–31 BC, commemorating each of the legions, proclaimed him as 'Antonius, Augur, *Triumvir* for the stabilising of the republic'. It is also worth noting that when, in 32 BC, the final battle-lines were being drawn between Antonius and Octavian, both the consuls in Rome, together with some 300 senators, left Rome to join Antonius in Greece: Octavian's dominance was not yet total.

The triumviral agreement lapsed at the end of 33 BC; this time Octavian needed no renewal. He was the head of a successful faction; consulships and proconsulships went to his supporters; he proclaimed himself the defender of traditional standards in national and family life. In the last months before war, Italian communities swore an oath of allegiance to him personally as leader; in this way, the whole of Italy effectively became part of his clientage, and his standing (*auctoritas*) rose immeasurably as a result. Although Octavian might try to portray the looming conflict as a righteous war in which traditional standards were being defended against the onslaught of oriental barbarism, the truth was otherwise. The battle of Actium, off the Greek coast, in 31 BC, was the final act in a struggle for dominance between rival faction leaders. In essence, therefore, it differed little from the factional crises that had been a regular feature of Roman political life since the mid-second century BC.

The victory that Agrippa won for Octavian in 31 BC set the final seal on the old republic; by 30 BC, both Antonius and Cleopatra were dead, and Octavian (the new Caesar) was the undisputed master of the Roman world, the victorious faction leader. The struggle in Roman politics between the primacy of the traditional forms of government and the domination of factional and individual ambition had finally been settled.

# EPILOGUE

Historians have seen the battle of Actium as a watershed – the end of the republic and the beginning of the Augustan *principate*. It is doubtful whether most Romans would have been aware of this great milestone, as Octavian, his faction and patronage represented a massive demonstration of continuity. Because of this, it was easy for such slogans as 'the restored republic' (*respublica restituta*), whatever they actually meant, to slip into the political vocabulary.

In a sense, of course, Octavian's victory at Actium was not the fall of the republic but a decisive stage in its evolution – decisive, because the Augustan *principate* that followed proved to be the way of supervising the *respublica* that had previously been so elusive. The evolution – some would say collapse – of the Roman republic had in fact been a process continuing and gathering momentum over at least the century before Actium. The traditional governmental instruments of the republic did not disappear but went on to be essential parts of the Augustan *principate*.

The change that characterised the gradual fall of the republic lay in the relationship between the instruments of government and the manner in which they worked. Their original forms had suited the needs of a small city-state with few external interests or responsibilities; they suited, too, a state in which it was thought perfectly appropriate that a relatively small group of people should, because of the contribution that their wealth enabled them to make, enjoy a virtual monopoly of power.

The concentration of power into the hands of a small oligarchic group did not change; its stability, however, was disturbed by the opportunities offered by a growing empire for members of this group to pursue individual visions and ambitions. Thus, individuals and factions came to see that they could exploit the republic's forms for their own needs, and at the expense of their peers. The means by which this could be done changed with time, but a decisive point was undoubtedly reached when these factions and individuals could count armies and kings amongst their clients. From then on, the fact that political and military power was vested in the same people made disorder and anarchy inevitable.

Many were obsessed simply with capitalising on this state of affairs; a few tried to find a way in which stability could be maintained, realised that the supervision of the republic had to be achieved, and saw that this was realistically open only to those who controlled the military power. The directness of approach exemplified by men like the Gracchi, Scipio Aemilianus, Marius, Catiline or Clodius proved intolerable to their peers; the openly authoritarian stances of Sulla and Caesar seemed for a while to offer hope, but, in the event, the hope was illusory because their domination removed from their peers a genuine opportunity to compete for honours and fulfil ambitions.

A voice that might have pointed a way through the *impasse* was that of Cicero; in his 'Union of the Orders' he recognised the need for a stability based upon a certain type of harmony and upon an ultimate guarantee of armed protection for that harmony. Perhaps because he was from a family of Italian origin, Cicero's vision was broader than most Romans could embrace, though it still lacked the breadth of a man like Julius Caesar, who took into account not only the ordinary people of Rome, for whom Cicero had little concern, but also the empire at large. Ultimately, Cicero was too constrained by the system, as is demonstrated by the fact that his great moments of effectiveness (63 and 44–43 BC) coincided with behaviour on his part that was in legal terms outrageous.

Cicero was, however, right in at least one important respect: the nobility would not tolerate obvious and institutional domination, and so control had to be exercised in a more subtle manner.

Although there is no suggestion that Augustus – the honorific name that Octavian was granted in 27 BC – modelled his *principate* on Ciceronian principles, he did share Cicero's appreciation that supervision had to be exercised with subtlety. For political and personal reasons, Pompey was an inappropriate choice on Cicero's part, but Cicero was right in believing that the *moderator* should be able to exercise his role through the strength of his personality, clientage and standing in the republic (*auctoritas*), rather than by virtue of any specific office that he might hold. Augustus' second settlement of the *principate* (23 BC) approached the problem in a not dissimilar way.

In this he based his own control on the tribunician power (*tribunicia potestas*) and an overriding and dominating military power (*imperium proconsulare maius*), though in practical terms he was neither a tribune nor a proconsul. He thus demonstrated his appreciation of where the seeds of the republic's management (and mismanagement) lay. He appreciated, too, both for his own security and for the stability of the republic, the need for a broad harmony; senators and equestrians were brought together as the two arms of a governmental and imperial service. Honours were open to competition, and elections were held as normal; Augustus' influence was exercised through a traditional form of canvassing which, because of his standing, was sufficient and successful. Thus, magistrates and promagistrates were dependent upon him, but not in an overt or humiliating fashion. Further, Augustus' control of the army was exercised through trusted individuals who emerged by means of this system.

Augustus was concerned, too, to occupy a traditional patronal role with regard to ordinary people; his building programmes provided work, and there was food and entertainment available to the urban plebs. Provincials, too, benefited from his expansion of Caesar's policies, so that Roman citizenship was for many a realistic goal, and the fear of rapacious officials was significantly lessened. With an emphasis on provincial prosperity and stability, armies could be kept to a size that was politically and economically acceptable: they certainly did not approach the huge numbers of which the triumvirs had disposed. This, in its turn, served to push into the background the ultimate military sanction that was, of course, his. It was important, too, that the army was made permanent, with regular terms of service leading to a retirement that was funded initially by Augustus himself but subsequently from taxation. This permanent army was stationed not near Rome but in the provinces where it was needed.

Augustus recognised also that the *respublica* did not consist simply of a set of political institutions: family life, traditional religious practices, the agricultural stability of the Italian small farmer – all came within the orbit of his patronal care. He was *pater patriae*, the national 'father-figure', the guarantor of peace, stability and the gods' continuing favour. After nearly half a century in power, by the end of his life Augustus was seen as indispensable to the continued well-being of the *respublica* – in many ways, a Ciceronian *moderator*.

The weakness of the Augustan system proved to be the manner in which he tried to secure its stability in the long term. Whilst in theory members of the senatorial nobility could aspire to a primacy like his, they lacked in practice the means to achieve it during his lifetime. Realising perhaps the dangers that threatened in a revival of factional squabbling amongst the nobility, including the type that had characterised his own triumviral relationship with Antonius, Augustus determined that the future should be secured within a dynastic framework, based upon his and Livia's families – the Julii and the Claudii.

The historian Tacitus saw this as the return of *dominatio*, and the later emperor Galba observed that the fact that Rome had in effect become the heirloom of Augustus' family represented an attack upon *libertas*. Whilst nobody would doubt the great capabilities of Augustus himself, the necessary blend of qualities was by no means obvious in Tiberius (AD 14–37), Caligula (AD 37–41), Claudius (AD 41–54) or Nero (AD 54–68). Their weaknesses, and particularly their inability to step directly into the shoes of Augustus, served to show that the dynastic approach required modification, and a way needed to be found by which *principatus* and *libertas* could be harmonised. Thus, by the end of the first century AD, in a manner that recalled the republic, every office, including at times the role of *princeps* itself, was open to any senator by the consensus of his peers.

However, despite the changes that occurred in the century after Augustus, his successors continued to see him as the ultimate source of their authority and as representing the standard by which they would be judged. Augustus' acknowledged success, both during his lifetime and subsequently, demonstrates how wrong Antonius had been when he dismissed Octavian as owing everything to his name: although it may have been unintentional in such a sarcastic comment, Cicero was nearer the mark in seeing Octavian as 'the divine youth', for it was he who in the *pax Augusta* guaranteed the survival of the Roman *respublica*.

# APPENDIX I

## PRINCIPAL DATES

BC 753 Foundation of Rome by Romulus (trad.)

753–509 Regal period (trad.)

509 Expulsion of Tarquinius Superbus; establishment of the republic (trad.)

494 Introduction of office of tribune of the plebs (trad.)

421 Quaestorship (and thus senatorial membership) opened to plebeians

367 Enactment that one consul each year should be a plebeian

339 Publilian law enacts sovereignty of the plebeian assembly

287 Hortensian law re-enacts the provision of the Publilian law

264–241 First Punic War; acquisition of first overseas provinces

218–202 Second Punic War; Hannibal's invasion of Italy

146 Destruction of Carthage and Corinth

145 (or 140?) Abortive land bill of Scipio's faction

137 Numantine War; Tiberius Gracchus' rupturing of relations with Scipio Aemilianus

133 Tribunate and death of Tiberius Gracchus

131 Italian 'cause' espoused by Aemilianus

129 Death (murder?) of Scipio Aemilianus

126 Expulsion of Italians from Rome

125 Abortive franchise bill of Fulvius Flaccus; revolt of Fregellae

123–122 Tribunates of Gaius Gracchus

121 Suicide of Gaius Gracchus

112 Outbreak of war in North Africa against Jugurtha

109 Metellus Numidicus in North Africa

107 Marius' first consulship; takes over conduct of the African War

105 Defeat of Jugurtha

102–101 Marius' fourth and fifth consulships; defeats inflicted on the Cimbri and Teutones

100 Marius' sixth consulship; *senatus consultum ultimum* passed against Saturninus and Glaucia

98 Caecilian-Didian law passed to prevent 'omnibus' legislation

| | |
|---|---|
| 95 | Expulsion of Italians from Rome |
| 91 | Tribunate and death of Marcus Livius Drusus |
| 91–88 | Social War |
| 88 | Sulla's first consulship; legislation of Sulpicius Rufus; Sulla's first march on Rome |
| 87–83 | Sulla in the east; war against Mithridates |
| 87 | Massacre of *optimates* at the hands of the Marians |
| 86 | Marius' seventh consulship |
| 82 | Sulla's second march on Rome |
| 81–79 | Sulla's dictatorship and constitutional reforms; proscription programme |
| 79 | Sulla's resignation |
| 77 | Catulus and Pompey put down revolt of Lepidus |
| 77–73 | Pompey in Spain |
| 73–71 | Revolt of Spartacus; return of Pompey |
| 70 | Joint consulship of Pompey and Crassus; dismantling of Sulla's constitution |
| 67 | Gabinian law gives Pompey the command against the pirates |
| 66 | Manilian law gives Pompey the command against Mithridates |
| 65 | So-called 'first Catilinarian conspiracy' |
| 63 | Consulship of Cicero; abortive legislation of Rullus; Catilinarian conspiracy; death of Mithridates |
| 62 | Pompey's return from the east; Clodius and the *Bona Dea* affair |
| 60 | Formation of first triumvirate of Pompey, Crassus and Caesar |
| 59 | Caesar's first consulship; Clodius' transfer to the plebs |
| 58 | Tribunate of Clodius; banishment of Cicero |
| 58–49 | Caesar in Gaul |
| 57 | Recall of Cicero from exile; Pompey's corn commission |
| 56 | Gang warfare in Rome; renewal of the triumvirate at Lucca |
| 55 | Second joint consulship of Pompey and Crassus |
| 54 | Death of Julia |
| 53 | Death of Crassus at Carrhae |
| 52 | Murder of Clodius; anarchy in Rome; Pompey appointed 'sole consul'; Pompey's marriage to Cornelia |
| 50 | Discussion of Caesar's position in Gaul; tribunate of Curio |
| 49 | Caesar's crossing of the Rubicon |

| | | |
|---|---|---|
| | 49–45 | Civil war |
| | 48 | Defeat of Pompey at Pharsalus; Pompey murdered later in Egypt |
| | 46 | Suicide of Cato |
| | 44 | Caesar made *dictator perpetuus*; murder of Caesar (Ides of March) |
| | 43 | Battle of Mutina; second triumvirate of Antonius, Octavian and Lepidus; proscription of Cicero |
| | 42 | Battles of Philippi; suicides of Brutus and Cassius |
| | 41–40 | Perusine War against Lucius Antonius |
| | 40 | Treaty of Brundisium patching up second triumvirate |
| | 39 | Treaty of Misenum with Sextus Pompeius; return of republican 'exiles' |
| | 38 | Octavian's marriage to Livia |
| | 37 | Treaty of Tarentum; renewal of the second triumvirate |
| | 36 | Defeat and death of Sextus Pompeius; disgrace of Lepidus |
| | 36–32 | Preparations for war between Octavian and Antonius |
| | 34 | 'Donations of Alexandria' |
| | 31 | Battle of Actium |
| | 30 | Suicides of Antonius and Cleopatra |
| | 27 | First settlement of the Augustan *principate* |
| | 23 | Second settlement of the Augustan *principate* |
| AD | 14 | Death and deification of Augustus; accession of Tiberius as the first Julio-Claudian successor |

# Appendix II

## MAGISTRACIES OF THE ROMAN REPUBLIC

**Consul**   Two **consuls** elected annually by the *comitia centuriata*; both had *imperium* (power of military control), and were recognised as the chief military and political executives of the state, the tenure of the **consulship** generally being regarded as the apex of a political career (save perhaps for the censorship). The **consuls** would command armies in the field, preside over the *comitia* and the senate, and they proposed laws to the people (*ius agendi cum populo*). They theoretically had rights of jurisdiction, though in criminal cases this was generally delegated, and civil jurisdiction was taken over by the **praetor urbanus**. Each was attended by twelve lictors. (After 367 BC, at least one consul had to be a plebeian.)

**Praetor**   The office may have gone back to the regal period, though it appears to have been 'reinvented', probably in 367 BC, and possibly as a way of answering the concession of that year which gave one of the annual **consulships** as of right to a plebeian. A **praetor** was elected each year with special responsibility for civil jurisdiction (**praetor urbanus**): but he, and his later colleagues, possessed *imperium* and could properly act as army commanders and preside over the assemblies and senate and introduce business to them. The **praetor**'s *imperium*, however, was inferior to that of the **consul** and had to yield before it, and he was attended by only six lictors. In 242 BC, a second **praetor** was added to deal with civil jurisdiction between citizens and foreigners (**praetor peregrinus**). Two further **praetors** were instituted in 227 BC with responsibility respectively for Sicily and Sardinia, so that there were four **praetors** elected annually by the beginning of the second Punic War. Two more were instituted in 197 BC to govern the two provinces of Spain, and the number was raised to eight by Sulla and to sixteen by Julius Caesar. **Praetors** were elected in the *comitia centuriata*.

The **praetor urbanus** had the duty of publishing an *edict* stating the principles according to which he proposed to administer justice, and these edicts were the cumulative source of much Roman law in later times.

The **consulship** and the **praetorship** were the only two regular magistracies that carried *imperium*; but there was provision for the *imperium* of a **consul** or **praetor** to be prolonged (*prorogatio*), and, in later times, certainly from Sulla onwards, it was in virtue of such prolonged *imperium* that ex-**consuls** and ex-**praetors** (known usually as proconsuls) governed provinces. It also sometimes happened that a special grant of *imperium*, specified as consular, praetorian or proconsular, might be conferred on a named individual (as with Scipio Africanus in 210 BC, and more notably with Augustus after 31 BC).

**Dictator**   There was provision in an emergency for a **consul** to nominate a **dictator** with overriding *imperium*, who was to hold office only for six months or for the duration of the emergency, whichever was the shorter; a **dictator** was attended by twenty-four lictors. (According to these rules the dictatorship of Sulla and most of Caesar's tenures of the office in the 40s BC were irregular.)

The **dictator**, in addition, had the right to appoint his deputy, the *Master of the Horse*, and to delegate his *imperium* to him – the only instance according to regular procedure of a holder of *imperium* being allowed to delegate that *imperium* to another without reference to the people; the practice was extended when Pompey (who was never **dictator**) was allowed in 67 BC and also in 55 BC to appoint deputies with *imperium*, and when Augustus was allowed to appoint his own deputies to govern provinces.

**Censor**   Two ex-magistrates elected by the *comitia centuriata*, generally every five years, holding office only until their functions were performed, and anyway for not more than eighteen months. Their primary task was to revise the list of citizens, ensure their proper registration, and assess the value of their property and their 'moral worth'. To this was added a review of the membership of the senate in which they could enrol new members, and remove any who seemed morally unworthy. A **censor** could not be called to account for his actions as **censor**. Although the office did not carry *imperium*, it was regarded as the most august of magistracies, and its holders were almost always ex-**consuls**.

**Aedile**   Four elected annually, of whom two were 'curule' aediles, two 'plebeian' aediles. Strictly only the **curule aediles** were magistrates, elected by the *comitia tributa*, the **plebeian aediles** being elected by the plebs alone, in the *concilium plebis*. The functions of the two kinds of **aediles** were, however, apparently indistinguishable. They had a general responsibility for maintenance in the city of Rome, a *cura urbis* (maintaining roads, water supply, etc.), a responsibility to maintain the corn supply (*cura annonae*), and they were expected to lay on magnificent games. They also had some limited powers of jurisdiction in minor matters.

**Quaestor**   The most junior magistracy; originally two were appointed by the **consuls** as their assistants. The number was increased to four and made subject to election, traditionally in 421 BC. From about 267 BC, there were eight **quaestors**, until Sulla increased the number to twenty. Of the eight in office in the third and second centuries BC, two were **quaestores urbani**, whilst two were expected to assist the **consul** in the field. They clearly had financial responsibilities. Elected by the *comitia tributa*, ex-**quaestors** automatically (after Sulla) became members of the senate.

## PLEBEIAN OFFICES

**Tribune of the plebs**   Ten elected annually; they had sacrosanctity (personal inviolability), the right and duty of bringing help to a citizen being arrested by a magistrate (*ius auxilii ferendi*), the right to veto the action of a magistrate (thus for instance stopping the levy or stopping a motion being put to the vote of the senate or *comitia*), and the right to convene and put proposals to the *concilium plebis*, whose resolutions (*plebiscita*), at least after 287 BC, had the force of law. Thus, in effect, they had the right to propose laws. (Sulla tried to restrict the tribunate's effectiveness by preventing its holders from proceeding to further office.)

**Plebeian aedile**   See under **aedile**.

## *CURSUS HONORUM* (SEQUENCE OF OFFICES)

The usual order of offices for a politically ambitious person was: **quaestor** (probably at minimum age of about 28), **aedile** or **tribune of the plebs, praetor, consul**. Two-year gaps were required between offices, though it seems that the aedileship/ tribunate could be missed out. The age requirements were stiffened by Sulla as follows: **quaestor**, 30; **praetor**, 39; **consul**, 42. It was further enacted by Sulla that not more than one magistracy could be held at a time by the same man; nor could a man hold the same office twice within a ten-year period (both rules being broken by Sulla himself).

# APPENDIX III

## THE VOTING ASSEMBLIES OF THE REPUBLIC

| | Comitia curiata | Comitia centuriata | Comitia tributa | Concilium plebis |
|---|---|---|---|---|
| Composition voting units | 30 curiae, 10 each from 3 ancient tribes | 193 centuries – 18 cavalry, 170 infantry (arranged in the ratio 80, 20, 20, 20, 30, according to 5 property classes), 5 of unarmed (i.e. unpropertied) citizens | 35 tribes | 35 tribes |
| citizens attending | each curia represented by one man (a lictor) | all citizens | all citizens | plebeians only |
| presiding officer | consul or praetor or (for religious purposes) chief priest | consul or praetor | consul or praetor or curule aedile | tribune of the plebs or plebeian aedile |

| *Duties* | | | | |
|---|---|---|---|---|
| elections | | consuls, praetors, censors | curule aediles, quaestors, lower officers, special commissioners | tribunes and aediles of the plebs |
| legislative | confirmed *imperium* of magistrates; confirmed adoptions and wills | (until about 218 BC, chief law-making body); subsequently used for declaration of war, confirmation of powers of censors | all types except those restricted to *comitia centuriata* | all types except those restricted to *comitia centuriata*; decisions (known as *plebiscita*) had force of law after 287 BC |
| judicial | | capital charges (increasingly after 150 BC limited to treason charges) | all crimes against the state which were punishable by fine (after the time of the Gracchi, these duties increasingly lost to the other courts) | |

# APPENDIX IV

# THE PROVINCES OF THE ROMAN EMPIRE

## PROVINCES AND DATES OF CREATION

| | | |
|---|---|---|
| BC | 241 | Sicily |
| | 238 | Sardinia; Corsica |
| | 198 | Hispania Tarraconensis and Baetica |
| | 167(?) | Illyricum |
| | 146 | Africa |
| | | Macedonia |
| | 133 | Asia |
| | 121 | Transalpine Gaul |
| | 100(?) | Cilicia |
| | 89 | Cisalpine Gaul (northern Italy) |
| | 74 | Cyrene |
| | 67 | Crete |
| | 63 | Bithynia-Pontus |
| | | Syria |
| | 58 | Cyprus |
| | 51 | Gallia Lugdunensis |
| | | Gallia Belgica |
| | (31 | Battle of Actium) |
| | 30 | Egypt |
| | 27 | Aquitania |
| | | Achaea |
| | 25 | Galatia |
| | 16 | Lusitania |
| | 15 | Raetia |
| | | Noricum |
| | 14 | Cottian Alps |
| | | Maritime Alps |
| AD | 6 | Moesia |
| | | Judaea |
| | 10 | Pannonia |
| | 12 | Germania Superior |
| | | Germania Inferior |
| | 17 | Commagene |
| | | Cappadocia |
| | 40 | Mauretania Caesariensis |
| | | Mauretania Tingitana |

43      Britain
        Lycia
        Thrace
106     Dacia
        Arabia
114     Armenia
115     Mesopotamia
        Parthia

# SELECT BIBLIOGRAPHY

## I A NOTE ON THE CLASSICAL SOURCES

Some of our information comes from later classical authors; of these, the most significant is Plutarch (c. AD 120), whose Roman biographies are collected in two volumes in Penguin Classics – *Makers of Rome* and *The Fall of the Roman Republic*. Besides Plutarch, considerable use is made of the historical writings of Appian (c. AD 150), Dio Cassius (c. AD 220) and of Suetonius' *Life of Caesar* (c. AD 120). These are, of course, in various ways dependent upon earlier authors, some of whom survive in fragmentary form. It is clear, however, that whilst the late republic could be an attractive subject for early imperial writers, it could also be one that tested the sensibilities of Augustus' successors; Cremutius Cordus, writing during the reign of Tiberius, was prosecuted for praising Brutus and Cassius. Perhaps the greatest loss amongst authors of this kind is represented by the later books of Augustus' friend, the historian Livy, to whom Augustus is said to have referred as 'my Pompeian friend'.

Much contemporary or near-contemporary writing survives and is available in Penguin Classics; these include many of Cicero's forensic and political speeches, though we have to bear in mind that the published versions usually represent Cicero's own later 'working-up' of the originals, so that what survives may be what he would have liked to have said rather than what he did say; his surviving speech in defence of Titus Annius Milo (on trial for the murder of Clodius) is a celebrated example of this. Most importantly, a very large collection of Cicero's *Letters* survives, and is available in Penguin Classics. The collection was put together after Cicero's death by his former slave, Tiro, and *may* have been subject to some censorship by Octavian and Antonius. A selection of Ciceronian passages relating to the management of the republic is translated by W.K. Lacey and B.W.J. Wilson in *Res Publica* (Oxford: Oxford University Press, 1970). Caesar's accounts of the *Gallic War* and the *Civil War* are available, as are Sallust's monographs on the *Jugurthine War* and the *Catilinarian Conspiracy*. Sallust's *Histories*, however, survive only as fragments.

## II MODERN AUTHORITIES

There are numerous books which cover the period of the late Roman republic; most of these will be cited in the general bibliography, but the fullest coverage of the subject matter contained in the present book is provided by the *Cambridge Ancient History*, vol. IX:

J.A. Crook, A. Lintott and E. Rawson (eds), *The Last Age of the Roman Republic, 146–43 BC*, Cambridge: Cambridge University Press, 1994.

# GENERAL BIBLIOGRAPHY

## Abbreviations

*Class. Phil.*     Classical Philology
*JRS*          Journal of Roman Studies

F.E. Adcock, *Roman Political Ideas and Practice*, Ann Arbor: University of Michigan Press, 1959.

F.E. Adcock, *Marcus Crassus, Millionaire*, Cambridge: Heffer, 1966.

A.E. Astin, *The Lex Annalis before Sulla*, Brussels: Collection Latomus 32, 1958.

A.E. Astin, *Scipio Aemilianus*, Oxford: Oxford University Press, 1967.

A.E. Astin, *Cato the Censor*, Oxford: Oxford University Press, 1978.

E. Badian, *Foreign Clientelae*, Oxford: Oxford University Press, 1958.

E. Badian, *Roman Imperialism in the Late Republic* (second edition), Oxford: Oxford University Press, 1968.

E. Badian, *Publicans and Sinners: Private Enterprise in the Service of the Roman Republic*, Oxford: Blackwell, 1972.

J.P. Balsdon, *Julius Caesar and Rome*, Harmondsworth: Pelican Books, 1967.

J.P. Balsdon, *Life and Leisure in Ancient Rome*, London: Bodley Head, 1974.

M. Beard and M.H. Crawford, *Rome in the Late Republic: Problems and Interpretations* (second edition), London: Duckworth, 1999.

K.R. Bradley, *Slavery and Society at Rome*, Cambridge: Cambridge University Press, 1994.

D.C. Braund (ed.), *The Administration of the Roman Republic*, Exeter: Exeter University Press, 1988.

T.R.S. Broughton, *The Magistrates of the Roman Republic* (2 vols), New York: American Philological Association, 1951–52.

P.A. Brunt, The Roman Mob, *Past and Present* 35 (1966), 3–27.

P.A. Brunt, *Italian Manpower*, Oxford: Oxford University Press, 1971.

P.A. Brunt, *Social Conflicts in the Roman Republic*, London: Routledge and Kegan Paul, 1971.

P.A. Brunt, *The Fall of the Roman Republic*, Oxford: Oxford University Press, 1988.

T.F. Carney, *Gaius Marius*, Chicago: Argonaut, 1970.

B. Caven, *The Punic Wars*, London: Weidenfeld and Nicolson, 1980.

M.L. Clarke, *The Noblest Roman*, London: Thames and Hudson, 1981.

T.J. Cornell, *The Beginnings of Rome, 753–263 BC*, London: Routledge, 1995.

M.H. Crawford, *Roman Republican Coinage*, Cambridge: Cambridge University Press, 1974.

M.H. Crawford, *The Roman Republic* (second edition), London: Fontana Press, 1992.

K. Dowden, *Religion and the Romans*, Bristol: Bristol Classical Press, 1992.

A. Drummond, *Law, Power and Politics: Sallust and the Execution of the Catilinarian Conspirators*, Stuttgart: Franz Steiner, 1995.

D.C. Earl, *Tiberius Gracchus: A Study in Politics*, Brussels: Collection Latomus 66, 1963.

D.C. Earl, *The Moral and Political Tradition of Rome*, London: Thames and Hudson, 1967.

H. Flower (ed.), *The Cambridge Companion to the Roman Republic*, Cambridge: Cambridge University Press, 2004.

E. Gabba, *Republican Rome: The Army and the Allies*, Berkeley and Los Angeles: University of California Press, 1976.

J.F. Gardner, *Being a Roman Citizen*, London: Routledge, 1993.

M. Gelzer, *Caesar: Politician and Statesman*, Oxford: Blackwell, 1968.

M. Gelzer, *The Roman Nobility*, Oxford: Blackwell, 1969.

A.K. Goldsworthy, *The Roman Army at War, 100 BC–AD 200*, Oxford: Oxford University Press, 1996.

A.M. Gowing, *The Triumviral Narratives of Appian and Cassius Dio*, Ann Arbor: University of Michigan Press, 1992.

M. Grant, *Julius Caesar*, London: Weidenfeld and Nicolson, 1969.

P. Greenhalgh, *Pompey* (2 vols), London: Weidenfeld and Nicolson, 1981.

E.S. Gruen, *The Last Generation of the Roman Republic*, Berkeley and Los Angeles: University of California Press, 1974.

E.S. Gruen, *Culture and National Identity in Republican Rome*, London: Duckworth, 1993.

M. Hadas, *Sextus Pompey*, New York: Columbia University Press, 1930.

W.V. Harris, *War and Imperialism in Republican Rome*, Oxford: Oxford University Press, 1979.

K. Hopkins, *Conquerors and Slaves*, Cambridge: Cambridge University Press, 1978.

N. Horsfall, *The Culture of the Roman Plebs*, London: Duckworth, 2003.

E.G. Huzar, *Mark Antony: A Biography*, Minneapolis: University of Minnesota Press, 1978.

A. Keaveney, *Sulla: The Last Republican*, London: Croom Helm, 1982.

A. Keaveney, *Lucullus: A Life*, London: Routledge, 1992.

L.J.F. Keppie, *The Making of the Roman Army: From Republic to Empire*, London: Batsford, 1984.

J. Leach, *Pompey*, London: Croom Helm, 1978.

A.W. Lintott, P. Clodius Pulcher – Felix Catilina?, *Greece and Rome* 14 (1967), 157–169.

A.W. Lintott, Cicero and Milo, *JRS* 64 (1974), 62–78.

A.W. Lintott, Electoral Bribery in the Roman Republic, *JRS* 80 (1990), 1–16.

A.W. Lintott, *Imperium Romanum*, London: Routledge, 1993.

A.W. Lintott, *Violence in Republican Rome* (second edition), Oxford: Oxford University Press, 1999.

A.W. Lintott, *The Roman Republic*, Stroud: Sutton Publishing, 2000.

A.W. Lintott, *The Constitution of the Roman Republic*, Oxford: Oxford University Press, 2003.

K. Lomas, *Roman Italy, 338 BC–AD 200*, London: Routledge, 1996.

R. MacMullen, *Roman Social Relations*, New Haven, Conn.: Yale University Press, 1974.

J.B. McCall, *The Cavalry of the Roman Republic*, London: Routledge, 2001.

C. Meier, *Caesar*, London: Fontana Press, 1996.

F.G.B. Millar, The Political Character of the Classical Roman Republic, 200–151 BC, *JRS* 74 (1984), 1–19.

F.G.B. Millar, Politics, Persuasion and the People before the Social War, *JRS* 76 (1986), 1–11.

F.G.B. Millar, Political Power in mid-Republican Rome, *Curia* or *Comitium?*, *JRS* 79 (1989), 138–150.

F.G.B. Millar, *The Crowd in Rome in the Late Republic*, Ann Arbor: University of Michigan Press, 1998.

T.N. Mitchell, *Cicero: The Ascending Years*, New Haven, Conn.: Yale University Press, 1979.

R. Morstein Marx, *Mass Oratory and Political Power in the Late Roman Republic*, Cambridge: Cambridge University Press, 2003.

H. Mouritson, *Plebs and Politics in the Late Roman Republic*, Cambridge: Cambridge University Press, 2001.

C. Nicolet, *The World of the Citizen in Republican Rome*, London: Batsford, 1980.

J.A. North, Politics and Aristocracy in the Roman Republic, *Class. Phil.* 85 (1990), 277–287.

R.M. Ogilvie, *The Romans and their Gods*, London: Chatto and Windus, 1969.

R.M. Ogilvie, *Early Rome and the Etruscans*, London: Fontana Press, 1976.

T.W. Potter, *Roman Italy*, London: Guild Publishing, 1987.

A. Powell and K. Welch (eds), *Sextus Pompeius*, London: Duckworth, 2002.

J.W. Rich, The Supposed Roman Manpower Shortage of the Later Second Century, *Historia* 32 (1983), 287–331.

J.S. Richardson, *Roman Provincial Administration*, Bristol: Bristol Classical Press, 1994.

J.S. Richardson, *The Romans in Spain*, Oxford: Blackwell, 1998.

E.T. Salmon, *Roman Colonisation Under the Republic*, London: Thames and Hudson, 1970.

H.H. Scullard, *Scipio Africanus: Soldier and Politician*, London: Thames and Hudson, 1970.

H.H. Scullard, *Roman Politics, 220–150 BC*, Oxford: Oxford University Press, 1973.

H.H. Scullard, *A History of the Roman World, 753–146 BC* (fourth edition), London: Methuen, 1980.

H.H. Scullard, *From the Gracchi to Nero* (fifth edition), London: Methuen, 1988.

R. Seager (ed.), *The Crisis of the Roman Republic*, Cambridge: Cambridge University Press, 1969.

R. Seager, *Pompey: A Political Biography*, Oxford: Blackwell, 1979.

A.N. Sherwin-White, *The Roman Citizenship* (second edition), Oxford: Oxford University Press, 1973.

A.N. Sherwin-White, The Political Ideas of Gaius Gracchus, *JRS* 72 (1982), 18–31.

R.E. Smith, *Service in the Post-Marian Army*, Manchester: Manchester University Press, 1958.

P. Southern, *Marc Antony*, Stroud: Tempus, 1998.

E.S. Staveley, *Greek and Roman Voting and Elections*, London: Thames and Hudson, 1972.

D. Stockton, *Cicero: A Political Biography*, Oxford: Oxford University Press, 1971.

D. Stockton, *The Gracchi*, Oxford: Oxford University Press, 1979.

R. Syme, *The Roman Revolution*, Oxford: Oxford University Press, 1939.

R. Syme, *Sallust*, Cambridge: Cambridge University Press, 1964.

D. Taylor, *Cicero and Rome*, London: Macmillan, 1991.

L.R. Taylor, *Party Politics in the Age of Caesar*, Berkeley and Los Angeles: University of California Press, 1949.

L.R. Taylor, *Roman Voting Assemblies from the Hannibalic War to the Dictatorship of Caesar*, Ann Arbor: University of Michigan Press, 1966.

Note. In 1957, a volume was published commemorating the 2000th anniversary of Caesar's assassination (*Greece and Rome* 4); it contains a number of significant papers.

F.W. Walbank, *Polybius*, Berkeley and Los Angeles: University of California Press, 1972.

A.E. Wardman, *Rome's Debt to Greece*, London: Elek, 1976.

R.D. Weigal, *Lepidus: The Tarnished Triumvir*, London: Routledge, 1992.

S. Weinstock, *Divus Julius*, Oxford: Oxford University Press, 1971.

C.R. Whittaker, *Rome and Its Frontiers*, London: Routledge, 2004.

T. Wiedemann, *Cicero and the End of the Roman Republic*, London: Duckworth, 1994.

M.M. Willcock, *Cicero: The Letters of January to April 43 BC*, Warminster: Aris and Phillips, 1995.

Ch. Wirszubski, *Libertas as a Political Idea at Rome*, Cambridge: Cambridge University Press, 1950.

T.P. Wiseman, *New Men in the Roman Senate, 139 BC–AD 14*, Oxford: Oxford University Press, 1971.

T.P. Wiseman, *Roman Political Life, 90 BC–AD 69*, Exeter: Exeter University Press, 1985.

Z. Yavetz, *Plebs and Princeps*, Oxford: Oxford University Press, 1969.

Z. Yavetz, *Julius Caesar and his Public Image*, London: Thames and Hudson, 1983.

# INDEX OF PERSONS AND PLACES

Actium, Battle of 10, 94, 97, 98

Aemilius Lepidus, Marcus (cos 78) 47

Aemilius Lepidus, Marcus (cos 46) 64, 90, 92, 93, 94, 96

Aemilius Paullus, Lucius (cos 182) 27

Africa 24, 25, 36, 37, 38, 41, 55, 92, 94, 96

Agrippa (s.v. Vipsanius)

Alexander 'the Great' 40

Alexandria 86, 96

Allobroges 58

Alps 24

Annius Milo, Titus (tr. pl. 57) 69, 74

Antonius, Gaius (cos 63) 56, 67

Antonius, Lucius (cos 41) 94

Antonius, Marcus (pr. 74) 49

Antonius, Marcus (cos 44) 1, 56, 64, 77, 82, 88, 89, 90, 91, 92, 93, 94, 95, 96, 97, 101

Appian 72

Appuleius Saturninus, Lucius (tr. pl. 103) 38, 42, 44

Aquae Sextiae, Battle of 38

Ariovistus 66

Arpinum 37, 53, 56, 60

Asia (Roman Province) 36, 40, 50, 52, 65

Asia Minor 40, 53, 78, 93, 97

Asinius Pollio, Gaius (cos 40) 64

Athens 88

Attalus III 33

Augustus (Emperor, 31 BC–AD 14) 1, 3, 4, 8, 10, 11, 26, 64, 73, 81, 88, 90, 91, 92, 93, 94, 95, 96, 97, 98, 100, 101, 102

Aurelia (m. of Caesar) 49

Aurelius Cotta, Lucius (cos 65) 55

Aurelius Cotta, Marcus (cos 74) 50

Autronius Paetus, Publius (pr. 68) 55

Bacchus (Dionysus) 26

Baetica 24

Balbus (s.v. Cornelius)

Bibulus (s.v. Calpurnius)

Bithynia 50, 52

*Bona Dea* 60

Britain 73

Brundisium (Brindisi) 94, 95

Brutus (s.v. Junius)

Caecilius Metellus Creticus, Quintus (cos 69) 52

Caecilius Metellus Nepos, Quintus (cos 57) 59

Caecilius Metellus Numidicus, Quintus (cos 109) 37

Caecilius Metellus Pius, Quintus (cos 80) 47

Caecilius Metellus Pius Scipio, Quintus (cos 52) 73, 74

Caelius Rufus, Marcus (tr. pl. 52) 76, 77, 79

Caesar (s.v. Julius)

Caesarion 86, 96

Calpurnius Bibulus, Marcus (cos 59) 62, 65, 67, 69, 74, 88

Calpurnius Piso, Gnaeus 54

Calpurnius Piso, Lucius (cos 58) 68

Campania 20, 65

Carrhae, Battle of 73

Carthage 1, 22, 23, 24, 25, 30, 36

Cassius Longinus, Gaius (tr. pl. 49) 77, 80, 88, 91, 93

Catiline (s.v. Sergius)

Cato (s.v. Porcius)

Catulus (s.v. Lutatius)

Caudine Forks, Battle of 22

Cicero (s.v. Tullius)

Cilicia 40, 50, 52, 76, 77

Cimbri 37f, 65

Cinna (s.v. Cornelius)

Claudia (d. of Appius Claudius Pulcher) 31

Claudius (Emperor, AD 41–54) 21, 84, 101

Claudius Marcellus, Gaius (cos 50) 77

Claudius Marcellus, Marcus (cos 51) 75f

Claudius Nero, Tiberius (pr. 42) 95

Claudius Pulcher, Appius (cos 143) 31

Claudius Pulcher, Appius (cos 54) 15

Claudius Pulcher, Gaius (cos 177) 31

Cleopatra 78, 86, 94, 95, 96, 97

Clodius Pulcher, Publius (tr. pl. 58) 15, 52, 60, 61, 67, 68, 69, 70, 71, 72, 74, 83, 99
*Comitia Centuriata* 7, 14ff, 41, 65, 110f
*Comitia Curiata* 10, 14ff, 110f
*Comitia Tributa* 14ff, 39, 41, 44, 110f
Comum (Como) 76
*Concilium Plebis* 6, 7, 11, 14ff, 33, 35, 36, 37, 39, 41, 44, 65, 68, 110f
Corfinium / Italica 39
Corinth 25, 30
Cornelia (m. of the Gracchi) 31
Cornelia (d. of Metellus Scipio) 73
Cornelius, Gaius (tr. pl. 67) 51
Cornelius Balbus, Lucius (cos 40) 88
Cornelius Cinna, Lucius (cos 87) 41, 42
Cornelius Scipio Aemilianus, Publius (cos 147) 3, 31, 33, 34, 59, 99
Cornelius Scipio Africanus, Publius (cos 205) 24
Cornelius Scipio Nasica, Publius (cos 138) 33
Cornelius Sulla, Lucius (cos 88) 4, 10, 30, 37, 39, 40ff, 46, 47, 49, 50, 51, 52, 54, 55, 57, 58, 61, 68, 69, 80, 82, 91, 93, 99
Cornelius Sulla, Publius (pr. 68) 55
Cornelius Tacitus, Publius 1, 3, 101
Corsica 23, 94
Cotta (s.v. Aurelius)
Crassus (s.v. Licinius)
Crete 52
Curio (s.v. Scribonius)
*Cursus honorum* 10, 44, 68, 109
Cyprus 69

Danube, river 87
Decidius Saxa, Lucius 95
Domitius Ahenobarbus, Lucius (cos 54) 71, 72

Egypt 25, 54, 67, 70, 78, 86
Epirus 12, 22
Etruscans 5, 20, 21, 39

Falerii Novi (S. Maria di Falerii Novi) 23
Falerii Veteres (Civitacastellana) 23
Faliscans 23, 35
Fregellae (Monte Cassino) 35
Fulvius Flaccus, Marcus (cos 125) 35, 36, 37

Gabinius, Aulus (cos 58) 51, 52, 53, 66, 71
Galba (Emperor, AD 68–69) 101
Gaius Caligula (Emperor, AD 37–41) 101
Gallia Cisalpina 66, 76, 91
Gallia Transalpina 66, 91
Gaul 20, 21, 58, 66, 72, 73, 75, 81, 84, 85, 86, 88, 93, 94
Glaucia (s.v. Servilius)
Gracchus (s.v. Sempronius)
Greece 3, 6, 22, 25, 78, 93, 97

Hamilcar Barca 23f
Hannibal 24, 25, 31
Helvetii 66
Hirtius, Aulus (cos 43) 92
Hispania Tarraconensis 24
Horace (Quintus Horatius Flaccus) 11, 26

Illyricum 66
Italy 8, 13, 18, 19, 20, 21, 22, 23, 24, 26, 27, 31, 34, 35f, 37, 38, 39, 40, 42, 44, 49, 59, 65, 72, 77, 78, 84, 91, 93, 94, 95, 96, 97

Jugurtha 37
Julia (d. of Caesar) 66, 73
Julia (d. of Augustus) 94
Julius Caesar, Gaius (cos 59) 4, 10, 45, 46, 47, 49, 56, 58, 59, 62, 63, 64, 65, 66, 67, 69, 70, 71, 72, 73, 74, 75, 76, 77, 78, 79ff, 90, 91, 92, 93, 95, 96, 99, 100
Junius Brutus Albinus, Decimus (pr. 45) 92
Junius Brutus, Lucius (cos 509) 88
Junius Brutus, Marcus (tr. pl. 83) 47
Junius Brutus, Marcus (pr. 44) 80, 88, 89, 91, 93
Junius Pennus, Marcus (tr. pl. 126) 35
Juvenal (Decimus Junius Juvenalis) 26, 45, 59

Laelius, Gaius (cos 140) 31, 33, 59
Lars Porsenna 20
Latins 20, 21, 36, 39
*Leges Publiliae* 13, 16
Lentulus Spinther, Publius (cos 57) 71
Lepidus (s.v. Aemilius)
*Lex Campana* 65, 71

*Lex Cornelia Annalis* 10, 44, 51, 91
*Lex Gabinia* 53
*Lex Hortensia* 13, 16
*Lex Manilia* 53
*Lex Pompeia de Provinciis* 74f, 76
*Lex Vatinia* 72
*Lex Villia Annalis* 10
Licinius Crassus, Marcus (cos 70) 49,
    50, 51, 52, 54, 60, 62, 63, 64, 68,
    70, 71, 72, 73, 92
Licinius Crassus, Publius 73
Licinius Lucullus, Lucius (cos 74) 42,
    50, 51, 52, 53, 54, 61
Livia Drusilla 95, 96, 101
Livius Drusus, Marcus (tr. pl. 91) 39
Livy (Titus Livius) 8, 20
Lucca 72
Lucceius, Lucius (pr. 67) 62
Lucullus (s.v. Licinius)
Lutatius Catulus, Quintus (cos 78) 47,
    85
Lycia 40

Macedonia 24, 25, 90, 91
Magistracy 8ff, 100, 106ff
Manilius, Gaius (tr. pl. 66) 52, 53
Manlius Torquatus, Lucius (cos 65) 55,
    56
Manlius, Gaius 58
Marius, Gaius (cos 107) 4, 37ff, 40, 41,
    42, 44, 47, 53, 99
Matius, Gaius 82, 87
Mediterranean 2, 22, 24, 40, 49, 51, 52,
    53
Messius, Gaius (tr. pl. 57) 71
Metellus (s.v. Caecilius)
Misenum 95
Mithridates VI 40, 41, 42, 49, 50, 51, 52,
    53
Mutina (Modena), Battle of 92

Neapolis (Naples) 20, 95
Neptune 92
Nero (Emperor, AD 54–68) 101
Nicomedes 50
Nola 40, 41

Octavia 94, 95
Octavian (s.v. Augustus)
Octavius, Gnaeus (cos 87) 41
Octavius, Marcus (tr. pl. 133) 53

Opimius, Lucius (cos 121) 37
Oppius, Gaius 88
Ostia 20, 85

Pansa (s.v. Vibius)
Papirius Carbo, Gaius (cos 120) 34
Parthia 73, 95
Pergamum 25, 33, 36
Perusia (Perugia), Battle of 94
Pharsalus, Battle of 78, 80, 82, 88
Philip V 24, 25
Philippi, Battles of 93
Picenum 46
Piso (s.v. Calpurnius)
Plutarch 31, 72
Po, river 19, 20, 39, 54
Polybius 3, 6, 7, 8, 24, 45, 60
Pompeii 44
Pompeius Magnus, Gnaeus (cos 70) 4,
    42, 46ff, 64, 65, 66, 67, 68, 69, 70,
    71, 72, 73, 74, 75, 76, 77, 78, 79, 80,
    83, 86, 88, 91, 92
Pompeius Strabo, Gnaeus (cos 89) 46,
    55
Pompeius, Sextus 92, 93, 94, 95, 96
Pomptine Marshes 85
Pontus 40, 42
Porcius Cato, Marcus (cos 195) 27
Porcius Cato 'Uticensis', Marcus
    (tr. pl. 62) 12, 58, 60, 61, 62, 67, 68,
    69, 74, 84, 86, 87, 88, 91
Ptolemy Auletes 67, 70, 78
Publilius Philo, Quintus (cos 339) 16
Pyrrhus 12, 22

Rabirius, Gaius 59
Rhine, river 66
Rhodes 25, 49
Rome 1, 3, 4, 5, 7, 8, 14, 16, 19, 20, 23, 31,
    44, 46, 47, 57, 72, 73, 74, 84, 85, 93,
    96
    *Basilica Aemilia* 28
    *Basilica Iulia* 85
    *Basilica Porcia* 28
    *Basilica Sempronia* 28
    Capitoline Hill 8, 85
    Colline Gate 42
    *Forum Iulium* 85, 86
    *Forum Romanum* 28, 38, 55
    Jupiter, Temple of 8
    Mars the Avenger, Temple of 93

Tiber, river 20, 85
Venus Genetrix, Temple of 86
Roscius Amerinus, Sextus 43
Rubicon, river 77
Rullus (s.v. Servilius)

Sallust (Gaius Sallustius Crispus) 12, 54,
    58, 87
Samnites 20, 21
Sardinia 23, 92, 94
Saturninus (s.v. Appuleius)
Scipio (s.v. Cornelius)
Scribonia 95
Scribonius Curio, Gaius (tr. pl. 50) 76,
    77
Sempronius Gracchus, Gaius (tr. pl.
    123–2) 4, 28, 30, 35ff, 38, 40, 42,
    44, 45, 75, 99
Sempronius Gracchus, Tiberius (cos
    177) 27, 31
Sempronius Gracchus, Tiberius (tr. pl.
    133) 4, 30, 31ff, 42, 45, 53, 99
Senate 11ff
Sergius Catilina, Lucius (pr. 68) 12, 54,
    55, 56, 57, 58, 59, 60, 61, 69, 82, 99
Sertorius, Quintus 42, 47
Servilius Glaucia, Gaius (tr. pl. 101) 38,
    42, 44
Servilius Rullus, Publius (tr. pl. 63) 56
Sestius, Publius (tr. pl. 57) 69
Sicily 22, 23, 28, 49, 92, 93, 94
Spain 24, 31, 42, 47, 50, 51, 53, 54, 62, 72,
    73, 75, 94
Spartacus 50, 51
Suebi 66

Sulla (s.v. Cornelius)
Sulpicius Rufus, Publius (tr. pl. 88) 40,
    41, 42
Syria 71, 72

Tacitus (s.v. Cornelius)
Tarentum (Taranto) 22, 96
Teutones 37f, 65
Tiberius (Emperor, AD 14–37) 95, 101
Torquatus (s.v. Manlius)
Transpadanes 39, 54
Tullia (d. of Cicero) 87
Tullius, Servius 15, 20
Tullius Cicero, Marcus (cos 63) 12, 13,
    15, 27, 43, 46, 49, 51, 53, 54, 55, 56,
    57, 58, 59, 60, 61, 62, 66, 67, 68,
    69, 70, 71, 72, 75, 76, 77, 79, 80, 81,
    82, 84, 87, 88, 90, 91, 92, 93, 99,
    100, 101, 102
Tullius Cicero, Quintus (pr. 62) 77, 79
Tunisia 24

Varro (Marcus Terentius Varro) 62
Vatinius, Publius (cos 47) 64, 65, 66
Veii 20
Vercellae, Battle of 38
Vercingetorix 73, 75
Verres, Gaius (pr. 74) 49, 51
Vestals 60
Vettius, Lucius 68
Vibius Pansa, Gaius (cos 43) 92
Vipsanius Agrippa, Marcus (cos 37) 91,
    94, 96, 97

Zama, Battle of 24

# Routledge History

### Augustus Caesar
### 2nd Edition
David Shotter

History sees Augustus Caesar as the first emperor of Rome, whose system of ordered government provided a firm and stable basis for the expansion and prosperity of the Roman Empire. Hailed as 'restorer of the Republic' and regarded by some as a deity in his own lifetime, Augustus was emulated by many of his successors. David Shotter reviews the evidence in order to place Augustus firmly in the context of his own times. Key topics discussed include:

- the background to Augustus Caesar's spectacular rise to power
- his political and imperial reforms
- the creation of the *Respublica* of Augustus
- the legacy Augustus Caesar left to his successors.

Revised throughout, the second edition of this successful book takes the most recent research in the field into account. David Shotter also includes more coverage of the social and cultural aspects of this complex character's reign together with an expanded guide to further reading.

Hb: 0–415–31935–8     Pb: 0–415–31936–6

### Caligula
Sam Wilkinson

Sam Wilkinson provides an accessible introduction to the reign of Caligula, one of the most controversial of all the Roman Emperors. Caligula's policies have often been interpreted to be those of a depraved tyrant. This study provides a reassessment of this controversial reign by scrutinising the ancient literary sources that are so hostile to Caligula, and by examining the reasoning behind the policies he enforced.

With a guide to primary and secondary sources, a chronology and a detailed glossary, *Caligula* is an invaluable study of the reign of this fascinating Emperor.

Hb: 0–415–35768–3     Pb: 0–415–34121–3

Available at all good bookshops
For ordering and further information please visit:
## www.routledge.com

# Routledge History

## Emperor Constantine
## 2nd Edition
### Hans Pohlsander

*Emperor Constantine* provides a convenient and concise introduction to one of the most important figures in ancient history. Taking into account the historiographical debates of the twentieth and twenty-first centuries, Hans A. Pohlsander:

- describes the Roman world into which Constantine was born
- assesses Constantine's ability as a soldier and statesman
- emphasizes the significance of Constantine as Rome's first Christian emperor
- discusses the importance of the establishment of the new capital of Byzantium
- gives an even-handed assessment of Constantine's achievements.

This second edition is updated throughout to take into account the latest research on the subject. Also included is a revised introduction and an enlarged bibliography.

Hb: 0–415–31937–4     Pb: 0–415–31938–2

## Alexander the Great
## 2nd Edition
### Richard Stoneman

From a respected author in the field, this second edition has been updated throughout and provides the only concise introduction to the career and impact of this great Macedonian conqueror and the main themes of his reign.

Using primary and modern sources, along with archaeological and numismatic evidence, Richard Stoneman takes recent research and the current state of research on the Persian Empire into consideration, and sheds new light on this influential figure.

With an expanded bibliography, a new index and illustrations, this excellent book will not only fascinate students, it will prove to be an invaluable resource as well.

Hb: 0–415–31931–5     Pb: 0–415–31932–3

Available at all good bookshops
For ordering and further information please visit:
## www.routledge.com

# Routledge History

### Nero
### 2nd Edition
David Shotter

The reign of Nero is often judged to be the embodiment of the extravagance and corruption that have, for many, come to symbolise ancient Rome. David Shotter provides a reassessment of this view in this accessible introduction to Nero, emperor of Rome from AD 54 to AD 68. All the major issues are discussed including:

- Nero's early life and accession to power
- Nero's perception of himself
- Nero's domestic and international policies
- the reasons for Nero's fall from power and its aftermath.

This new edition has been revised throughout to take account of recent research in the field. Also included is an expanded bibliography and a new index.

Hb: 0–415–31941–2      Pb: 0–415–31942–0

### Athenian Democracy
### 2nd Edition
John Thorley

The fifth century BC witnessed not only the emergence of one of the first democracies, but also the Persian and the Peloponnesian Wars. John Thorley provides a concise analysis of the development and operation of Athenian democracy against this backdrop. Taking into account both primary source material and the work of modern historians, *Athenian Democracy* examines:

- the prelude to democracy
- how the democratic system emerged
- how this system worked in practice
- the efficiency of this system of government
- the success of Athenian democracy.

Hb: 0–415–31933–1      Pb: 0–415–31934–X

Available at all good bookshops
For ordering and further information please visit:
## www.routledge.com

# Routledge History

### Roman Britain
### 2nd Edition
David Shotter

The occupation of Britain by the Roman Empire for 400 years is still the subject of much interest and continually emerging material. *Roman Britain* by David Shotter introduces this period, drawing on the wealth of recent scholarship to explain the progress of the Romans and their objectives in conquering Britain. Key topics discussed include:

- the Roman conquest of Britain
- the evolution of the frontier with Scotland
- the infrastructure the Romans put in place
- the place of religion in Roman Britain.

Updated throughout to take account of recent research, this second edition includes an expanded bibliography and a number of new plates which illustrate the various aspects of the Roman occupation of Britain.

Hb: 0–415–31943–9    Pb: 0–415–31944–7

### Tiberius Caesar
### 2nd Edition
David Shotter

David Shotter provides a concise and accessible survey of the character and life of Tiberius Caesar, heir of Augustus Caesar and emperor of Rome from AD 14 to AD 37. *Tiberius Caesar* sheds light on many aspects of the reign of this enigmatic emperor, including the influential and often problematic relationships Tiberius maintained with the senate, his heir Germanicus and Sejanus. Other key topics discussed include:

- Tiberius's rise to power
- Tiberius's struggle to meet the demands of his role
- how far Tiberius's policies differed from those of Augustus
- why Tiberius retired from official duties in AD 26.

David Shotter has updated this second edition of *Tiberius Caesar* throughout, including a revised and expanded bibliography and a new index.

Hb: 0–415–31945–5    Pb: 0–415–31946–3

Available at all good bookshops
For ordering and further information please visit:
## www.routledge.com

# Routledge History

### Ancient Rome
### Sourcebook
Matthew Dillon and Lynda Garland

Experienced scholars, Lynda Garland and Matthew Dillon present an extensive range of material, from the Early Republic to the assassination of Julius Caesar.

Providing a comprehensive coverage of all important documents pertaining to the Roman Republic, Ancient Rome includes:
• source material on political developments in the Roman Republic (509–44 BC)
• detailed chapters on social phenomena, such as Roman religion, slavery and freedmen, women and the family, and the public face of Rome
• clear, precise translations of documents taken not only from historical sources, but also from inscriptions, laws and decrees, epitaphs, graffiti, public speeches, poetry, private letters and drama
• concise up-to-date bibliographies and commentaries for each document and chapter
• a definitive collection of source material on the Roman Republic.

All students of Ancient Rome and classical studies will find this text book invaluable at all levels of study.

Hb: 0–415–22458–6        Pb: 0–415–22459–4

Available at all good bookshops
For ordering and further information please visit:
## www.routledge.com

# eBooks

eBooks – at www.eBookstore.tandf.co.uk

## A library at your fingertips!

eBooks are electronic versions of printed books. You can store them on your PC/laptop or browse them online.

They have advantages for anyone needing rapid access to a wide variety of published, copyright information.

eBooks can help your research by enabling you to bookmark chapters, annotate text and use instant searches to find specific words or phrases. Several eBook files would fit on even a small laptop or PDA.

**NEW:** Save money by eSubscribing: cheap, online access to any eBook for as long as you need it.

### Annual subscription packages

We now offer special low-cost bulk subscriptions to packages of eBooks in certain subject areas. These are available to libraries or to individuals.

For more information please contact
webmaster.ebooks@tandf.co.uk

We're continually developing the eBook concept, so keep up to date by visiting the website.

## www.eBookstore.tandf.co.uk

CPSIA information can be obtained at www.ICGtesting.com
Printed in the USA
LVOW01s1247230114

370662LV00005B/162/P